Tipper.
The Photography of Dr.

...u Hemphill

Patrick Holland

Thalassa Books
Cahir, Co. Tipperary
2003

Introduction

I was appointed Curator of Tipperary S.R. County Museum in November, 1983. The museum then consisting of one room with myself as the staff. The small collection included Hemphill's volume of stereoscopic illustrations with its fine hand-illuminated dedication and intriguing photographs. I was impressed by the carefully chosen viewpoints and scenes. Prompted by an early visit by Mr. Eric Earle, Dr. Hemphill's great-grandson, I began to consider the possibility of an exhibition.

Years passed and the museum developed. We kept a constant watch for information about Dr. Hemphill. Some of my most exciting moments were when I recognised his work in an item brought to us. By the mid-1990's the museum and its holdings of Hemphill material had come to the point where an exhibition was possible. The approval of a project to construct a completely new county museum building gave an added impetus. A high quality exhibition of local interest was needed for our temporary exhibition gallery. I must put on record my appreciation of the support given by the Members, Management and staff of the local authorities in the county to the development of the museum.

The Hemphill exhibition was first seen by the public on the museum's opening day, 5th of May, 2000. I left the museum in April, 2002 to take up another post but brought with me a dream to make his images of Tipperary available to a wider audience.

Patrick Holland.

ISBN 0-9546448-0-8 Published byThalassa Books, Clonmel Road, Cahir, Co. Tipperary, Ireland.
Book and text © Thalassa Books 2003
Images © South Tipperary County Museum, 2003 (on its own behalf and on behalf of those who have given permission for reproduction to it).
Book designed by Creative Concepts
Printer Kilkenny Print

Acknowledgements

I would like to thank the following for their assistance: Mr. M. Ahern, The Nationalist newspaper of Clonmel, Mr. N. Shee, Mr. N. Cathcart, Lt. Col. J. Silcock, Mr. A.V. Dodge, Lord Rosse, Mrs. P. Rossiter, Mr. M. Girouard, the late Mrs. P. M. McDonough, Mr. J. Joyce, Ms. V. Dodier, Mrs. M. G. Darmody and the Local History Section of the County Library, Thurles, Mrs. M. Boland, Librarian and the staff of Clonmel Library, Mr. A. Wrixon, Mealy's Auctioneers, Ms. P. Hickey, Mr. and Mrs. O'Shea, Mr. P. O'Keefe, Professor M. Harker, Mr. D. Hemphill, Mr. P. Hemphill, Ms. S. Ball, National Botanic Gardens, Dublin, Ms D. Ireland, Royal Photographic Society, Bath, Ms. D. Maher, Mr. D. Davidson, Mr. J. Crowley, the staffs of the National Library of Ireland, The Royal Irish Academy and the National Museum of Ireland, Dr K. Kenefick of the Dept. of English, University College, Cork and many others. Mr and Mrs. E. W. D. H. Earle constantly encouraged me. I hope this book is a fitting acknowledgement in itself.

I want to thank all the staff who worked in the museum during my time there and Sarah Gillespie,the Curator and staff there now(especially Julia Walsh) who helped with the book. I am grateful to those who allowed the copying and reproduction of the images. I would like to thank my brother Michael for his careful proof reading, Ruth Maher, Yvonne Byrne and Geraldine Tobin for technical assistance and Ursula Mullins of Creative Concepts for her design work. I stole time from my family in Galway and from my wife Ellen and son Conor in Tipperary for this book and I hope the result is some small repayment.

I gratefully acknowledge the financial support of the Heritage Council under the 2003 Publications Grant Scheme.

All faults and errors are my own. I would be glad to learn of them and any further Hemphill works or information readers may come across.

Contents

"A Scholarly Gentleman", William Despard Hemphill, his life and interests.

William Despard Hemphill[1] was born into a large Tipperary Church of Ireland family in 1816. They were of the land-owning and professional middle classes. He was educated at the Clonmel Endowed School where the pupils were mostly Church of Ireland, the sons of army officers, merchants and the local gentry. The school's classical education prepared them for positions in the civil service, army, church or further study in university. W. D. H. followed his father, and other relatives, into the medical profession. His obituary notes that he pursued his medical profession *'with distinction ... and obtained his fellowship (of the Royal College of Surgeons) in 1844. In the latter year he took his degree of M.D. (at St. Andrews, Scotland[2]). He was for some years House Surgeon of the City of Dublin Hospital. At an early age he settled down in Clonmel ... Before long he was regarded as one of the leading practitioners of this district, being esteemed not alone a most skilful physician and surgeon, but also a true and faithful friend. During the course of his medical career in this town he was appointed Consulting Physician to the Clonmel District and Auxiliary Asylums, and also Visiting Physician of the Clonmel District Prison... was a very active member of the Royal Medical Benevolent Committee, and was for one year President of the Irish Medical Association[3]*.

In January, 1849 WDH. married Sarah Henrietta Pedder, a member of a prominent Clonmel legal and land-owning family. They had three children, Samuel William (1850-1901), Mary Beverley ('May') (1853-1925) and Evelyn Alice (1871-1892)[4]. Some years later WDH *'was said, by those who remembered him, to be a man of great personal charm[5]*. His obituary says *'The poor, too, without distinction, found in him a kindly-disposed and generous friend[6]*. May Hemphill's obituary described him as a *'scholarly gentleman whose name is still revered in this locality[7]*.

He was a man of strong religious views. He refers in his book, **Stereoscopic Illustrations** to the Church of Ireland's direct descent from pre-Patrician missionaries, subjugation by the Anglo-Normans to Rome and emancipation during the Reformation. He hoped that *'the faith, pure and unadulterated, ... be again the faith of her warm-hearted but benighted children[8]*. His brother, Richard was a theologian and may have influenced his religious views. WDH was a committed member of his church and was elected to the Diocesan Council and Synod and the General Synod[9].

WDH and his brother both had strongly Unionist political views. He notes in **Stereoscopic Illustrations** that the *'mild and benignant laws under which she (Ireland) is governed, give her more temporal freedom than perhaps any nation on the face of the earth'* [10]. He owned four houses in Johnston street and is said [11] to have refused to accept the nationalist Clonmel Corporation's renaming of Johnston street to honour Gladstone, the pro-Home Rule Prime Minister. He called them Brighton Place, a name they still hold. WDH's brother, Robert, was a conservative member of Clonmel Corporation from 1854 to 1858 and later opposed both church disestablishment and the Nationalist candidate in the general election of 1885[12].

Dr. Hemphill's father Samuel, and his uncle Richard, a lawyer, had lived at 12 Gordon Street (now Wolfe Tone Street), Clonmel in the 1820's-1830's. By 1856 his father is listed in Anne Street, a fine cul de sac of three storey houses. WDH is noted at Upper Johnston Street (Brighton Place). He seems to have kept his surgery there[13] for a while after he bought Oak Ville in 1871[14].

Oak Ville had been built in the mid-1820's by Henry Pedder, WDH's future father in law, as a residence for himself. It was situated in extensive grounds where the present-day shopping centre now stands, on the then northern outskirts of Clonmel. It was a two storey house of three bays, a shallow porch, a basement, a low pitched roof and wide eaves with a lower apparently slate hung wing to the rear. Its name came from the fact that its internal doors, staircase etc. were made of polished oak[15]. The nearby terrace of houses at Brighton Place and later owned by WDH was also constructed by Pedder at this time. In 1854 Oak Ville was described as suitable accommodation for *'a gentleman and his family, situated on a site in Upper Johnson Street of eight acres, with stables for ten horses, coach houses, cow houses and granaries'*[16]. WDH bought it from the widow of the Hon. George Ponsonby Prittie for £5,000[17]. Many of his later photographs are of the house and the garden.

W D H was a man of many interests and talents, both intellectual and practical. His obituary states that his *'was not an idle existence, but of useful and beneficent purpose... his constant preoccupations seemed never to produce a sense of weariness'*[18]. He clearly had an enquiring and active mind. He must have been possessed of determination and patience to persevere with hobbies such as photography and the growing of orchids.

Dr. Hemphill photographed the Library in Oak Ville in 1892. It was a cluttered masculine room, filled with a small grand piano, a billiards table, his microscope, a book case, its top shelf filled with what appears to be archaeological journals and a long glass fronted specimen case stacked full of geological specimens. The walls have several framed photographs or prints of scenic or architectural subjects while busts of composers, small statuettes, turned items and various dust catchers are on all the flat surfaces. They are the physical evidence for a busy life.

His interests in archaeology and historic architecture can be seen in the many views of sites among his photographs. While it was usual for the early photographers to have such subjects, Dr. Hemphill had a deeper interest. The descriptions of sites in his book show that he was capable of original research. He recorded the appearance of St. Mary's Church, Clonmel before it was altered by renovations[19]. The preface of his book notes his intention to preserve a record of the many beautiful and in some cases little known localities in his neighbourhood. He was a member of the then Kilkenny and South-East of Ireland Archaeological Society[20] and gave a Nuremburg jetton or token found at Clonmel to their museum[21].

WDH was also a talented musician. A press clipping reporting on a 'Toy Symphony Concert' held in the Parochial Hall, Clonmel, (Monday, 13th of January, possibly 1889 or 1890) noted that he not only played two flute solos with remarkable *'executant powers and ... thorough refinement as a musician ... with ... purity of tone and delicacy of expression'*, but was also the conductor of the orchestra and the composer of a march played at the concert. He was accompanied by Miss Evelyn Hemphill on violin and Miss Hemphill on drum and pianoforte. At an earlier concert held in May 1881, accompanied by Miss Hemphill, his performance was again praised. He also played a piece of his own composition, *'A Sprig of Shillelah'*[22]. His obituary notes that he reached high standards in music and gardening.[23] He exhibited his Boehm flute, made by Messrs. Rudall, Rose, Carte and Co. of London, at the Clonmel Art Exhibition of 1858[24].

WDH was an avid orchid grower with a large glass house and green house adjoining Oak Ville. Trees and plants are common subjects in his photography. He was a prominent member of the Clonmel Horticultural Society which *'had for many years- mainly due to his untiring exertions – a most flourishing existence'*[25]. In January 1854 he was one of three Trustees of the Society who leased a plot of land from John Bagwell to the north of the present Queen Street to add to their existing Horticultural Garden[26]. Some of his few known documentary photographs record a show at the Garden[27]. His interest in matters botanical lasted until his very old age. Among his latest known photographs are two views of the Botanical Garden in Dublin, which were published in 1897. They are reproduced in that institution's history[28]. It seems likely that WDH was familiar with that institution[29].

Ivory turning was another of WDH's interests. His daughter May's will[30] included a provision that her father's *'turned ivory ornaments, his own work exhibited in the London Exhibition of 1851'*[31] and his cabinet of geological specimens were to be given to the National Museum of Ireland. She died on the 31st of March, 1925. Among photographs held by the family is a one entitled *'Group of ivory turning - Great Exhibition. 1851'*[32]. There are over 20 items, all small decorative pieces, many of them cups and tazzas. Among the items on the lower shelf are what appears to be prize medals. He exhibited his ivory turning at the Clonmel Art Exhibition of 1858 while the Hon. Mrs Bagwell of Marlfield House exhibited a work box in sandal and African Blackwork turned by him. He even included his lathe, invented and made by W. T. Kennan of Fishamble Street, Dublin[33]. His interests stretched to criminal investigations. He published an 'Examination of Minute Bloodstains in Medico-Legal Investigations' in 1875. He describes four criminal cases in which his careful forensic examination had produced evidence used in prosecutions, some ending in the execution of the convicted person. He was clearly an astute and scientifically trained observer trusted by the authorities. We should add the *'geological research, ... microscopic investigations and discovery, as well as other matters'* noted by his obituary[34]. Girouard mentions that he was a collector of Waterford glass[35].

WDH suffered several losses and disappointments in later years. His son and he became estranged when Samuel made a marriage apparently seen by his father as unsuitable. Sarah Hemphill, his wife, died in November 1897. Her obituary noted that the deepest regret prevailed *'especially among the poorer classes of this district who retain a grateful sense of her benevolence, and many acts of kindness on their behalf*[36]. Their younger daughter, Evelyn Alice, had died earlier, in 1892. Samuel died in 1901, apparently while working as a music teacher in London though he seems to have attended medical school[37].

WDH worked on until he was in his early seventies and then retired, living with his only surviving child, May, at his house, Oak Ville[38]. He died on the 13th of July, 1902, aged 86. Cusack[39] noted that he had been blind for some years but an obituary[40] says that *'Up to two years ago he was in the enjoyment of unimpaired health but since then he gradually, almost imperceptibly declined… He retained his mental faculties in all their strength and clearness to the very latest moment of his existence'.* The obituary and report on the funeral were of sufficient interest to be reprinted specially by the Clonmel Chronicle[41], then a newspaper of conservative society in Clonmel[42]. The roll call of attendees at the large funeral (or those who sent their carriages) is a careful listing of the town's notables. He and his wife, two daughters and son are buried beneath a Celtic cross in the western portion of Old St. Mary's graveyard, Clonmel.

May Hemphill and WDH's granddaughter, Evelyn (Eva), Samuel's daughter, lived at Oak Ville until May's death in 1925. The house was left to Eva[43] but it was sold it as she had by then married a bank official and was living away from Clonmel. It was then described as a *'well appointed family residence, containing three reception rooms, ten bedrooms, large halls and landings, smoking-room, store-rooms, pantries, kitchens, … A greenhouse and hothouse open off the Dwelling-house. There is a fine walled garden stocked with fruit-trees, etc. There are three yards, stabling for eight horses, coach-houses, hay and straw lofts, cow and poultry houses. The grounds are well timbered with ornamental trees. Two tennis lawns, fountain, nice avenue and gate lodge within three minutes' walk of Railway Station, Post Office and Church.'*[44]

Some months later the store in Clonmel containing most of Oak Ville's contents was destroyed by fire. Thankfully the family photographic albums had been taken by Eva. Oak Ville, the grounds and orchard were sold to J.J. O'Shee, a solicitor and ex-Nationalist M.P. who lived there until he and his family moved back to Dublin in 1943. The house was divided into two and let to various tenants, one being Judge Troy, father of the novelist, Una Troy. By 1974 both parts were vacant. The roof was badly damaged by a storm in January and the house was then vandalised. The property was sold and the house was demolished on the 18th of October[45]. The shopping centre built on the site stands in the middle of what would have been the orchard, one wall of which remains between the centre and the school to the east.

Dr. Hemphill and Newtown Anner.

Dr. Hemphill was part of landed gentry society in Tipperary. Although he was a professional and a younger son, he came from a land owning family. His wife, Sarah Pedder, also gave him an entry to Big House and Clonmel establishment circles. He seems to have been particular friends with the officers in Clonmel barracks. There are several photographs of Royal Artillery officers, their wives, and Col. Eveleagh, the Barrack Master. Others are of gun crews in position, firing a salute and on camp at Lakefield and Marlfield[46]. His brother-in-law, H.B. Pedder, an officer in the 7th Huzzars, was also photographed in uniform.

WDH would have had shared interests, religious and political beliefs with the families of the local big houses. This gave him the opportunity to take photographs of the houses and, in some cases, of the owners. While he was obviously well known at Newtown Anner, he was also sufficiently welcome to take family photographs at Castletown Cox and Marlfield. The apparent lack of similar photographs of Gurteen or Kilmanahan Castle may indicate a lesser degree of familiarity with the families there. It may be that photography was a means of introduction to some of the houses.

There were very strong links between WDH and Newtown Anner. The house, its garden and the Osborne family are all prominent in his photography. The house is some three miles to the north-east of Clonmel, in the angle where the river Anner flows into the larger Suir. Slievenamon mountain is to the north-east and the Comeraghs to the south, across the Suir. Today Clonmel's houses and factories are creeping out towards Newtown Anner but in the 1850's the house and estate were deep in the countryside.

The Osbornes had held land in Co. Waterford since the seventeenth century. In 1739 Sir William Osborne had moved to Newtown Anner from Tickincor castle on the other side of the River Suir. His son, Sir Thomas, was also an M.P. but 'seems to have been remarkable for little except writing eccentric letters to the newspapers, shunning society and greatly enlarging the house at Newtown Anner between about 1798 and 1802'[47]. In 1816 Sir Thomas, then aged 58 returned to his house from England with his new bride, Catherine Smith, a beautiful girl aged nineteen or twenty[48]. He had met her in Brighton and although she and her family did everything possible to put him off, he insisted on proposing to her. She surprisingly eventually agreed. The gaps between them were pointed up when her family solicitor found it hard to accept the strange Irish names of the properties Sir Thomas was proposing to settle on his wife. A relative wrote that Catherine was acting *'under a mistaken notion of female vanity and of future grandeur'* Her suitor may have been an Irish eccentric but he was both rich and titled.

Lady Osborne lived a lonely life at Newtown Anner due to her husband's anti-social tendencies. There were few visitors and while the estate was a prosperous one, the house was quiet, *'no sound is to be heard but the cawing of the rooks and the echo of my own footsteps'*. She spent much of her time redesigning the gardens, especially during the Famine when she gave employment to many. She was an efficient manager of her estates after her husband's death. Lady Osborne died in 1856[49] having become very religious in later life[50]. Attempts to persuade the local Catholic peasantry of their religious errors were not appreciated.

Their one surviving child, Catherine Isabella, married Ralph Bernal[51] in 1844, and inherited the estate. They were substantial landowners: in 1878 Catherine had an estate of 12,242 acres and Ralph, 942 acres[52]. Ralph Bernal Osborne was a noted speaker in the House of Commons, Secretary to the Admiralty and sat for a number of different parliamentary constituencies. He

was active in famine relief committees in the Clonmel area. His career was described as 'His failure to reach those positions which his talents justified is due to his want of official industry and to the absence of that sobriety of judgement which is dear to the average Englishman'[53]. He seems to have been away in London a lot, enjoying himself as one of society's wits. She died in 1880 and he in 1882[54]. They had two children, Edith (1845-1926) and Grace (1847-1926).

The Hemphill family links with Newtown Anner seem to have begun with WDH's uncle, John, a surgeon who attended Sir Thomas on his deathbed[55] in 1821. If WDH also acted as the family doctor to the household, his relationship was more involved. He seems to have been a regular visitor there[56] and must have spent a good deal of his time photographing the house, the gardens and the family. His future father-in law, Henry Pedder, had also been a visitor to Newtown Anner, attending the celebration of Catherine Osborne's 21st birthday in 1839[57]. WDH was photographing Newtown Anner and the Osbornes in 1857 when he was thirty nine and Mrs. Osborne was thirty seven. They were obviously good friends. He 'attended Lady Osborne in her last illness, and his skill and kind friendship was a great comfort to her daughter during the trying time of her illness'[58]. Mrs. Osborne shared his interest in photography, owning two prints by Le Gray and had examples of his ivory turning[59]. Issue No. 9 of his **Stereoscopic Views of Clonmel and the Surrounding Country** was dedicated to her and Issue no.10 to R. B. Osborne. WDH dedicated his book, written in 1859, to her 'for her love of Everything Beautiful, in Nature or in Art, her warm admiration of Photography, or, her many private virtues, and endearing qualities, known best by those, who, like the author, have had the honour of her constant friendship, for many years'[60]. Dodier[61] regards Mrs. Osborne as his patron. His links with Newtown continued into the 1860's when he was photographing both Edith and Grace, as well as external and internal views of the house. His photographs were used to illustrate the two volume **Memorials of Lady Osborne** published in 1870[62]. It is unclear how long he remained in contact with the Osborne household. Presumably his relationship continued until the Bernal Osbornes died in the 1880's though he may not have continued his photography at Newtown Anner during all that time.

Edith and Grace Osborne posed many times for WDH and appear in some of his most beautiful photographs. They were known for their cleverness, beautiful hands and attractive voices. They grew up in ' a lively and educated household where (they) met many distinguished people' [63]. They were both talented artists and were encouraged by their mother, herself an artist. She had taken lessons from a Swiss artist during a tour on the Continent with her mother, Lady Osborne in 1833 [64]. Artists such as the English watercolorist, Thomas Shotter Boys (1803-1874) were invited to stay at Newtown Anner [65].

Edith was noted for her tall commanding figure and dark eyes, supposedly inherited from her father's Spanish Jewish ancestors. She was clearly a strong-minded girl. She eloped with Henry Arthur Blake, a police officer from a Galway family stationed in Clonmel, who was disliked by her parents because of his lack of a fortune [66]. However he had a very successful career, was knighted and was appointed Governor of several colonies. She is reputed to have spoken nine languages and to have guarded her husband with a revolver when he was a 'Special Magistrate' [67]. Despite his position, she had strong political interests and Anna Parnell, sister of Charles Steward Parnell, was one of her nationalist friends. Butler [68] notes of Lady Blake that her 'watercolours reveal her keen interest in plants and insects, and provide valuable scientific information, with her portrayal of both subjects being acutely accurate... Around the age of twenty, Edith became keenly interested in painting plants and insects. Throughout her life she travelled widely – largely due to the fact that her husband served as Governor of the Bahamas, Newfoundland, Jamaica, Hong Kong and Ceylon- recording the plant and insect life which she saw around her. She continued to paint until well into her seventies'. Could she have been influenced in her interest in plants by Dr. Hemphill ? She and her husband returned to live in Myrtle Grove, Youghal in 1907 and she died in 1926 [69].

Grace is also described as 'a competent and highly gifted artist who, perhaps because of social commitments, ... could not devote herself wholeheartedly to her art' [70]. A person who knew her described her as 'very pretty, quick and clever with perfect manners and the most attractive voice I have ever heard. She was kind-hearted, and though a perfect woman of the world, I never thought her worldly. Every man who knew her was in love with her and I am afraid she broke many hearts. .... She had both wit and humour' [71]. A Valentine card preserved at Hatfield House is as follows

Help me I pray ye muses mine
Your powerful aid I thus implore
To chose the fairest Valentine
For Eighteen hundred and sixty nine
The difficulty is, I ween,
Where all are wondrous nice and fair
To chose among them my heart's Queen

To reign supreme for all the year.
'Tis really puzzling to excess
Where Beauty starts at every turn
An embarras de vrai richesse
You scarce can choose for whom to burn

The Sankeys and their cousin Annie
The Quins, those charming sisters four
Bright Gina and her sister Fanny
The Mandevilles and Misses Moore

All these are very pretty ladies
Rich in great charms of form and face
But still not one of them, 'tis said is
Nice as Edith or Grace

Grace married the Duke of St. Albans and inherited Newtown Anner from her parents, Catherine and Ralph Bernal Osborne. The house descended through the St. Albans family until it was sold and its contents removed in 1987. Its present owner is restoring it.

Mark Girouard[72] describes it in modern times as follows, 'It was not a great house, but it had great charm, made up of many elements not all of which have been described: the wide-branched cedar and long views to the mountains in front of the house; the spacious white-washed stableyard and friendly kitchen court at the back; the railway line running through the kitchen court, by which wood and turf were carried into the house; the small dark book-lined rooms in the old wing, and the albums which their cupboards would disgorge, full of photographs of Victorian house parties, or letters from Dickens, Disraeli and other eminent Victorians; the Spy cartoons which jammed the walls of the gentlemen's lavatory, and the photographs of Silcock racehorses which replaced them; the dinner gong hanging between elephants' tusks at the foot of the stairs; the barrel-topped Irish chests which flanked the hall door, one filled to bursting with family papers; the wisteria and pineapple plants climbing around the fan light; and the doormat inscribed with 'welcome', a welcome which the house and its occupants never failed to give this writer for more than fifty years'.

"A More Truthful Likeness", William Despard Hemphill and photography.

In the early years photography was a hobby of the rich. Amateur photographers required time, education and financial means, as well as a knowledge of science and art. While WDH was a younger son in a large family, he had sufficient funds to pay for his hobby. He joined and eventually took over his father's practice. An obituary in the Nationalist [73] newspaper notes that he had a large and lucrative practice for many years as well as his position as doctor to the Prison and Asylum. At least one other Victorian doctor, Hugh Welch Diamond, took photographs[74] and clergymen amateurs were also known[75].

Photography had come to Ireland in the early 1840's. Two methods of reproducing an image, Daguerre's positive process and Talbot's negative process, had been made public in 1839, in France and England respectively. By October 1841 a commercial studio had been opened in Dublin [76]. In England 'photography was neither well known nor widely practised during the 1840's [77]. It became much more common after the Great Exhibition of 1851 in London where equipment and prints were on display. Stereographs became highly popular in the years after the Great Exhibition. These are photographs taken in pairs from slightly different angles which when viewed together give a three dimensional effect. In the same year the wet plate collodion negative process generally available to the public. The use of the wet collodion negative and the introduction of albumen coated paper in 1850 revolutionised photography, making both Daguerre and Talbot's processes obsolete. From 1880 the availability of dry plate gelatine negatives meant that negatives did not have to be developed on site and only the introduction of the Kodak camera and film in 1888 remained to make photography available to all.

The 3rd Earl of Rosse, of Birr Castle, was working with daguerreotypes in June 1842. His wife, Mary, Countess of Rosse, attended the Great Exhibition of 1851, took up photography late in 1853 and was active for a decade at least[78]. The relationship between WDH and Birr Castle is not clear but there is a signed example of his work there [79]. She may have acquired this as a result of her membership of the Amateur Photographic Association, having been elected in March, 1863.

Another photographer in the general area was Francis Edmond Currey, the Duke of Devonshire's land agent at Lismore Castle who was taking photographs of the castle and local people c. 1853 [80]. As with Lady Rosse, it is not possible to confirm any actual connection between Currey and Hemphill but there were links between the artistically inclined members of landed families [81].

Lady Hawarden, wife of Cornwallis Maude, Earl de Montalt and 4th Viscount Hawarden of Dundrum House [82] was another noted photographer with Tipperary connections. Like Currey and Hemphill, her place in photography is between the early amateurs of the 1840's and the professionals of the 1860's. Her work mainly consists of intense posed scenes in which her daughters, windows, mirrors and drapery are constant motifs [83]. Some appear to be reconstructions of events or stories from literature. There seems to be a strong influence from literature and art. Lady Hawarden is thought to have begun her photographic career in Dundrum in 1857 [84] and some of her early work shows scenes from there[85]. Her earlier work was with a stereo camera, as with Hemphill. Virginia Dodier, her biographer,[86] notes that she was never able to find any personal connection between WDH and Lady Hawarden. That he admired her work (which he could have seen on exhibition in London in 1863 and 1864, and in Dublin in 1865) is clear. But she did not spend that much time in Ireland after 1859'. She died in 1865 at the age of 42. As Dodier[87] writes, Dundrum House or the surrounding area are not among Hemphill's subjects nor does he dedicate any of his works to the family. This is important negative evidence as he photographed locations less than four miles from the Dundrum estate (at Athassel Priory and in Cashel). He also dedicated his works to a wide range of local upper class notables. This suggests that while he knew of Lady Hawarden, he did not know her personally or socially nor did he have any connection with her[88].

It is not possible, at present, to say where Dr. Hemphill learned photography. He attended St. Andrews university in the 1840's. At the same time Sir David Brewster, Principal of the University, 'was the nucleus of a very important group experimenting with the (calotype) process at St. Andrews[89]. This may be where he received his technical knowledge. The Osborne household may have been the source of his artistic education.

While his obituary notes that he was 'one of the first and most successful of amateur photographers'[90] it is difficult to precisely date the beginnings of his work[91]. A small under-exposed print in a family album[92] shows Lismore Castle with, in front, the bridge over the river. Scaffolding is visible and it would appear that the print records the temporary bridge or repair work undertaken after two arches collapsed in the flood of November, 1853[93]. This small under-exposed print is therefore a very early documentary photograph probably taken by WDH, given its provenance, and providing a start date for his work[94]. The images in **Stereoscopic Illustrations**, taken in 1857-8[95] are not as good as those of the 1860's but could still have had a year or more of experimentation beforehand. While it would be tempting to link a possible visit to the Great Exhibition of 1851 to his start in photography, a general date of the early years of the 1850's is more likely. He may taken photographs in South Tipperary for up to fifty years.

WDH's work can be divided into seven parts
1. Early work (single portraits and landscapes).
2. Stereoscopic images.
3. The St. Mary's Album.
4. Paper Albums issued before **Stereoscopic Illustrations**.
5. WDH's book, **Stereoscopic Illustrations**.
6. His later and probably best photographic work.
7. Final work including possible colour images.

1. Early Work (single portraits and landscapes).
Although WDH concentrated on posed or artistic views, there is some evidence that initially

he took both portraits and landscapes. Many of these single images, both views of places and portraits, may be prints from one of a pair of negatives. Some are identical or similar to views in his book. A single print image of 'Anner Castle', for example, is also known as a stereoscopic pair on a card[96]. An album inscribed 'Grace Osborne Scrap Book, Newtown Anner 11th April 1865' and now at Hatfield House contains some early portraits[97]. Three appear to date to the late 1850's to 1860, 'C. I. Osborne', a self-portrait of Dr. Hemphill and a portrait of Edith Osborne titled 'E.O. one of Dr. H's early attempts'. A second very small album, belonging to Grace Osborne [98] contains several portraits as well of views of Holy Cross and scenes in Italy and Killarney. While the latter and some of the portraits are probably commercial, two portraits, one of 'Jacceord', a servant at Newtown Anner [99] and the other 'Miss V Sauss' as well as views of Holy Cross, St. Mary's, Clonmel and Cashel are definitely by WDH. Other images of people such as one of a group which includes Capt. Meecor, Mrs. Hemphill, Mrs. Osborne and Miss Uniacke, or a family group of the Osbornes on the steps at Newtown Anner are probably by WDH as is a study of ornaments in the Sitting Room, Newtown Anner and a view of Anner Castle. The images in this album seem to date to between the mid-to late 1850's to the very early 1860's. They show that he was taking simple portraits, perhaps self-printed, of his social circle and servants at an early date in his photographic career.

2. Stereoscopic images

Stereoscopic images would appear to have been WDH's main and perhaps only method at the start. Although WDH is best known for the stereoscopic images in his book, a number of others are known. Some are domestic portraits[100]. Others relate to the Clonmel Art Exhibition (see below) or are of places photographed from different angles from the views in **Stereoscopic Illustrations**. Most were probably taken at the same time as those in **Stereoscopic Illustrations**, ie 1857-8. He used pre-printed paper mounts with ornate designs forming positions for the stereographs.

3 The St. Mary's Album

While **Stereoscopic Illustrations** is his best known work, it was not Dr. Hemphill's first or only photographic publication. In 1857 he recorded St. Mary's, Clonmel, his parish church before it was altered during restorations. He presented a booklet of these images, housed in a small leather wallet, to his brother[101]. The booklet is titled '**Photographic & Stereoscopic Views of St. Mary's Church, Clonmel taken in 1857 before the alterations and dedicated to John Bagwell J.P. by William D. Hemphill, M.D.**, published by William Curry & Co. Sackville Street and printed by Edmond Woods, Clonmel. There are eleven images, the first a frontispiece portrait of WDH, the second a reproduction of a printed title page with a frame and four circular views of St. Mary's.

The remaining nine images, two rectangular prints and seven stereoscopic pairs, are of the Church, both exterior and interior. The photographs seem to have been taken in spring or winter as there are no leaves on the trees. These photographs are of architectural value, as Hemphill himself intended. They show the church before the renovations of 1857[102]. Among the changes were the removal of the stepped battlements and the raising of the roof. Most of the views are architectural with some posed people. None approach the level of preparation and care seen in his later works. It is not clear how many copies of this publication existed but it seems unlikely to have been more than a few for family and friends.

4. Paper Albums issued before **Stereoscopic Illustrations**
The publication, as a single book, of **Stereoscopic Illustrations** was preceded by a series of twenty paper albums containing stereographs. Publication in parts was common at that time, following the way in which art prints were published[103]. An advertising leaflet for the paper albums is in the collections of the South Tipperary County Museum[104]. Although undated, it probably circulated sometime between the late 1850's and 1860 when **Stereoscopic Illustrations** was published. The albums contained four views, each surrounded by a 'beautiful enriched border, printed in gold, within a handsome cover'. The views could also be purchased mounted on 'green glazed card slides with gold borders and illuminated labels'. The views were printed in London with the cards and paper pages being printed by E. Wood in Clonmel. A copy of one

of these albums, no. 9, is in the collections of the County Museum [105]. It measures some 24.5 by 18.7 cm. It has a white glazed paper cover with an ornate printed frame in red and the title, in alternating green and red type.

This issue of no. 9 contains four stereoscopic pairs. Three, *'Kiltinan Castle'*, *'St. Patrick's Well and Old Church'*, and *'St. Patrick's Well near Clonmel'* are identical to those in **Stereoscopic Illustrations** though the fourth, *'Lady Osborne's Summer House, Newtown Anner'* is not. The pages have a printed gold foliage frame. When you compare this Part 9 and the later book, **Stereoscopic Illustrations**, there are differences. The list of numbers originally published in **Stereoscopic Illustrations** (Hemphill 1860, xix) describes issue nine as *'Kiltinan &c.'* The book however places the Kiltinan image in Chapter Eleven along with other *'Castellated Residences'*. Images of Newtown Anner are in Chapter Ten *'Scenery and County Seats'*. It may be that this particular issue of no.9 is an individual compilation[106].

The National Architectural Archive holds a copy of paper album no. 8 [107]. Two of the four images: No. 2 *'Scots Church, Clonmel'* and *'Model School, Clonmel'* are known from other collections, a third *'View of Clonmel from Merlin'* is similar to another but from a slightly different viewpoint and the fourth, *'Railway Station, Clonmel'*, taken from the road leading northwards to the railway bridge, is not known elsewhere. This album is therefore also different from the Clonmel section of **Stereoscopic Illustrations** as regards the number and subject of the images.

Single stereoscopic pairs mounted on card were also available as both the advertising leaflet and the cover of the Museum's copy of part no. 9 mention. The descriptions given 'green glazed card slides, with gold border and illuminated labels' matches some seen by the author [108]. However there are also definite WDH stereographs on card of different colours, cream for example, with many having the WDH monogram. There appear to be at least two printings of the cards as there are two versions of the foliage frame[109]. As with the paper parts and **Stereoscopic Illustrations** there appears to have been a good deal of variation due to re-issues, the individual wishes of Dr. Hemphill, his customers and perhaps those printing and pasting up the images. It may be that differing versions of the same general view were used, perhaps to speed up production by having two or more negatives at work at the same time. This means that WDH may have taken several views of a location.

It is clear that the stereoscopic and single images of this period, however they appear, on card, paper or in a book, are all derived from a greater whole, the collection of negatives taken by Dr. Hemphill. Some images appear only in one media but a broad range of family, topographic, antiquarian and artistic topics can be seen. While the camera and method had implications for quality, and while the subjects are not as carefully or artistically posted, the range of topics visible in his later high-quality work had been fully established by the publication of **Stereoscopic Illustrations** in 1860. Among the stereographs not in **Stereoscopic Illustrations** are ones of artworks exhibited at the Clonmel Art Exhibition of 1858, images from Newtown Anner, views of Clonmel, including one of his own house, externally and internally, in Johnston Street, Lismore Castle, views of family and friends, the Horticultural Garden and Clonmel Flower Show and St. Mary's[110]. Hemphill images seem to have circulated around his extended family and perhaps further afield[111].

5. WDH's book, **Stereoscopic Illustrations**
W.D.H is best known for his book, 'Stereoscopic Illustrations of Clonmel and the Surrounding County including Abbeys, Castles and Scenery with Descriptive Letterpress'[112]. The images were taken in 1857-8, the preface written in 1859 and the book published in 1860. It was published in Dublin by William Curry and Company, Upper Sackville-Street, Thomas Cranfield, Grafton Street and in London by A. W. Bennet, Bishopsgate-Street Without. WDH notes, in the conclusion, that the printing of the negatives has been entrusted to 'one of the most eminent photographic printers in London: J.A. Spencer, 6-7 Gold Hawk Terrace, Shepherd's Bush'.

The book is a large volume of cream pages with marbled end papers, text enclosed in printed red foliage frames and stereographs mounted within gold printed foliage frames with monogram. The title of the images is printed, in red, in a space in the frame below. The copy of the book held by South Tipperary County Museum has a leather cover obscuring spine decoration which seems to include interlace motifs. The page size is c. 30.8 x 20.4 cm and the pages have gilded edges. The book cost five guineas.

The County Museum's main copy[113] has a hand–illuminated dedication ' Sarah H Hemphill from WDH March 1866' [114]. It seems that WDH presented dedicated copies of the book to various members of his family several years after its publication [115]. The book is dedicated in print to 'To No One, Whether from her love of Everything Beautiful, in Nature or in Art, her warm admiration of Photography, or, her many private virtues, and endearing qualities, known best by those, who, like the author, have had the honour of her constant friendship, for many years, can this Volume of Illustrations of her own neighbourhood be more appropriately dedicated than to Mrs. Osborne, Newtown Anner, Clonmel'. He dates his work to the summers of 1857-8, mentions that he had, given his limited free time, to be content with the negatives he had obtained. He claims credit for being the first to use stereographs for book illustrations and the first to photograph in detail the antiquities and beauties of his neighbourhood[116]. As in his photography, he makes few mentions of contemporary events except in his references to the *'awful years of famine'* [117] and the relief work commissioned by Lady Osborne at Newtown Anner.

The book has a dedication, a preface, an introduction (to Clonmel and the surrounding area), a section dealing with his views on the introduction and progress of Christianity in Ireland, eleven illustrated sections and a conclusion. The eleven sections are Cashel, Holycross, Athassil (sic), Lismore, Mitchelstown, Ardfinnan, Cahir, Clonmel, Minor Antiquities, Scenery and Country Seats and finally Castellated Residences. Each section of the book is preceded by a short but detailed historical and antiquarian account of the location illustrated showing his strong interest in such matters. Some parts, such as that describing Holycross are original historical research. With the exception of the frontispiece, all of the photographs are stereographs. Most are square with rounded corners while oval prints were chosen for a few appropriate views. The frontispiece illustration is a full size print (24 cm x 19 cm) *'Cloictheach on the Rock of Cashel'* showing Dr. Hemphill standing by his camera in front of the Round Tower with another man sitting among the headstones. A small distant view of *'Clonmel from the Mountain'* is on the first title page. There are 80 illustrations contained within the eleven sections[118].
Recently the museum purchased a second copy of **Stereoscopic Illustrations**[119] at auction in England. It seems to be generally similar to the copy described above but there are significant differences[120]. There are several images which do not appear in the Sarah Hemphill's copy of the book[121]. Similar differences can be seen when her copy is compared to three other copies of **Stereoscopic Illustrations** which are still held by the family. Each is dedicated to a member of the family, one with the hand-written dedication *'To Richard Hemphill Esq. from his affectionate Nephew W. D. Hemphill, Clonmel, October 14th 1860'* probably given to his uncle on publication. The other two, with hand illuminated dedications, *'S. W. Hemphill from WDH 1866'* and *'M.B.F. Hemphill from W.D.H. 1866'* were given to his son and daughter six years later when they were aged fifteen and thirteen respectively. A quick comparison of the images in these albums found that there are differences
• between prints in the quality of printing,
• in the use of either a second version of the same location or
• in a magnified view of the same image or
• in a completely different image being used [122].
It is clear that there is variation between individual copies of **Stereoscopic Illustrations**. In effect each copy may be a unique compilation.

70. His later and probably best photographic work

WDH seems to have begun using a single large plate negative camera by 1860. He had enough work done and experience gained by 1862 to win an Honourable Mention for work submitted to the Great Exhibition in London. There are some dated photographs from 1860 and 1861 but the majority date from 1862 to 1867. This period seems to have been his most productive. He won several prizes. There are some differences in topic, photographs of the soldiers in the barracks being common here but not in the stereographs, as far as we know. However most subjects relate to his earlier work with, for example, monuments such as Cahir castle, views of Clonmel and area, studies from Newtown Anner all being common. The difference between his work of the 1850's and that of the 1860's is in terms of confidence and maturity. The posed scenes are carefully and patiently laid out. The viewpoints of the landscapes are meticulously selected. There is a masterful awareness of light and dark. In some ten years of photography, WDH's vision had matured, from exposure to the work of others or from a rigorous self-criticism. It became polished and assured. This could not have happened without an education in art or an environment in which art was appreciated.

7. Final work including possible colour images
The lack of dated images hints at a lull in the 1870's and 1880's. However it is likely that WDH continued his interest if not his actual involvement. Certainly there are photographs taken by him in the early 1890's. It seems that he and his daughter May had photography as a shared hobby in his retirement [123]. Among various items in the family's possession is a glass lantern slide, in colour, showing a woman, possibly May, seated beside the fountain in the garden of Oakville [124]. It is clear that either WDH or May were experimenting with early colour photography. May's obituary noted that her father was 'an early exponent of coloured photography, which he reduced to a fine art' [125].

Motivation, Themes, Influences and Methods
Dr. Hemphill's views on photography are recorded in a lecture he gave as part of the Clonmel Art Exhibition of 1858. A visiting exhibition of art from the South Kensington Museum was combined with local exhibits [126]. He was a committee member and exhibitor at the Art Exhibition[127]. He notes in the lecture that photography was well represented in the exhibition. He gives an outline of the history of the science, as he calls it, up to then, and of the various chemical processes involved including collodion. He had been in contact with Mr. Skaiffe[128] who had sent him two photos.

He then discusses the uses of photography and makes it clear that he values photography as a way of sending images of their relatives to the *thousands of our fellow-countrymen exiled in Australia and America ... While I will not pretend to rank them (photographs) as works of art beside the production of the Great Masters, for my own part I would prefer the photographs of Claudet or Mayall*[129] *and a host of others, as giving a more truthful likeness and retaining the peculiar identity of those I loved, to the finest portraits of Lawrence or Reynolds or the exquisite miniatures of Thorburn and Ross. I now of course speak of first-rate photographic likenesses'.* He discusses landscape photography and notes two beautiful examples in the exhibition as well as the *'so many really good landscapes annually ... on the walls of our Photographic Exhibitions'.* He then goes on to say that *'all agree that it (photography) excels all other arts in the perfection of its architectural pictures'* and mentions some examples on display. The use of photography to copy works of art for educational purposes and for medical purposes are also noted. He finishes up the short talk by mentioning stereographs but deplores the reconstructed scenes with *'vulgar groups of pretended home-scenes and hawking parties, with stuffed animals and pasteboard back-grounds, which abound in every shop window, not to speak of those whose demoralising influence is so great, that one does not know which to wonder most at, - the possibility of procuring models, as they are called, or that such things should be* tolerated or encouraged by a Christian public. Not that I would be understood to cast a slur on pic-nics, weddings, and tea-parties, providing the subjects are pure and the accessories natural'. His views on photography were informed by his own interests, high aesthetic standards, strong moral and religious beliefs and a concern for others, such as those exiled by emigration.

The preface of **Stereoscopic Illustrations**, written the following year, records Dr. Hemphill's intention to 'illustrate by sun-pictures the beauties within easy access of his home, to pass agreeably the few holidays he had and to preserve a record of the many beautiful and in some cases little known localities in the neighbourhood'. He is clear that one of the book's aims was to encourage others to visit the scenery around Clonmel. His pride in the locality and its scenery is obvious. He noted that he photographed subjects chosen for their historical and archaeological value rather than for 'mere qualities that would render them more attractive to the admirer of picturesque beauty'[130].

While WDH's motivation in taking photographs seems to have been varied it is consistent with his social standing and beliefs. He aimed to record historical sites for posterity, to bear testimony to his religious beliefs, his appreciation of plant and artistic images and to instruct the viewer. His position within the upper classes is unquestioning and supportive of the established order. While he was certainly affected by suffering, and approved, for example, of the charitable works undertaken at Newtown Anner to give employment, poverty and deprivation do not appear in his photographs. Photography was for him a means to record the beautiful: diversions into documentary subjects were not a occasion for social comment. His work started some ten years after the Famine but there is no sign of pain or poverty in his photography. He was not a radical but a charitable and principled gentleman scholar of his time. For him photography was an artistic pursuit, not a record of ordinary life.

While we can see some development of topics, the differences are mainly due to a growing expertise, maturing artistic vision and changes in methods and equipment. His work seems to have followed the same pattern of development as photography in general some years before. At first it was enough to simply record the world about. When the creative desire to produce works of art arose, the existing modes in art (tableaux, still lives etc) were copied. Later generations would move on, after the heights of the art photography of the 1860's and 1870's, to create new visions for the medium.

Certain basic themes can be seen in **Stereoscopic Illustrations**. His antiquarian and religious interests coincide in his many views of medieval ecclesiastical sites such as the Rock of Cashel, Holycross Abbey, Athassel Priory and Donaghmore Church. There are fewer archaeological sites of purely 'secular' interest such as the Cromleac at Gurteen or the castles at Ardfinnan and Cahir.

Contemporary churches are featured but only those of the Church of Ireland. General views of towns, taken from a height, are notable as are scenic views of bridges, water and trees. While there are some of people arranged in a landscape, most photographs containing people are those of Big Houses whose occupants he would have known (Newtown Anner or Marlfield, for example). He photographed both local Big Houses and castellated residences, the latter being attractive as architectural sites as well as the residences of friends or acquaintances. Scenic features in demesnes such as Cahir Cottage (now the Swiss Cottage) or the bridge beside it also feature. Purely documentary urban views such as no. 49 showing the Scots' Church and Anglesey Street, Clonmel are rare[131]. He does give a good deal of attention to public buildings such as the Model School or the Railway Station in his home town but not in other towns. He notes in the conclusion that views of Coumshingaun, the huge glacial lake in the Comeragh Mountains and of many other places well worthy of illustration were been omitted due to lack of space. It is interesting to note that although he went as far as County Cork and deep into Co. Waterford he does not seem to have photographed further west than Cahir or further north than Holycross.

Many of his later images are repeat (and better) attempts of locations photographed in **Stereoscopic Illustrations**. But there are additional themes such as the biblical tableaux and the portraits of friends and families. These may not be new themes however as we may be missing earlier work [132]. His images show the work of someone with very strong ideas as to what is an appropriate subject. Views of architectural monuments show his interest in light, shadow and form. He had a strong creative urge and this, backed by a visual education and appreciation of art, resulted in works such as *'The Slope'*. His other interests such as gardening figure strongly as does a technical interest in photography itself shown by experimental images such as *'Judith with Holofernes' head. 1864'* and others stressing sharply focused detail. His self-image as a 'man of taste' is evident in his images of works of art, both in the 1858 Clonmel Art Exhibition Catalogue and also in his views of Big House interiors. These Big House photographs show the Victorian love of possessions but there is a deeper meaning. His friendship with the Osborne family of Newtown Anner may have been his entry point into upper class society but perhaps photography was another means of moving within it. He was a member of Tipperary's Church of Ireland and Unionist establishment and a staunch conservative. Many of his photographs could be seen as an identification with tradition, continuity and the established order.

Documentary photographs do not figure very prominently in his known work. There are some, such as *'Firing Royal Salute from New Bridge. Clonmel. Queen's Birthday. 1864'*, *'District Lunatic Asylum, Clonmel 1863'* or best of all *'Flower Show, Clonmel, April 1863'* but these all relate directly to other interests or aspects of his work rather than as pure documentation. While people figure prominently in many of his photographs, many are there as figures in the landscape, an idealised landscape of peasants and scenic views, as French art of the period saw it. Others are there as figures in a tableau, scenes inspired by his religious beliefs. Such genre photographs 'dependent on a strong fictional story line, usually with a moral and executed in a formal, composed and painterly manner' were common subjects with amateur photographers [133]. Few are as intimate and as emotionally committed as the views of his daughter or his son

though even here there are personal messages. May has fallen asleep reading her father's book. Samuel is playing a musical instrument showing perhaps not only his interest in music but his father's. In most of WDH's photographs he is setting the scene and determining the messages transmitted. Some of the early photographs which may have been taken by WDH are more direct and intimate[134] and he has some fine portraits in his later work, for example those of his brother in law, H. B. Pedder or Colonel Eveleagh, but in most cases, his portraits show people submissively looking away or down. Few return the photographer's gaze.

The subjects of WDH's photographs are not unusual in the context of the early photographers. English amateurs of the 1850's followed Talbot in their subjects: 'historic monuments, landscapes, still lives, pictures of beautiful objects and reproductions of works of art[135]. Among the meanings of these images is the confirmation of the traditional values of the landed gentry and professional classes. The income, leisure time and interests of the upper classes allowed them to be the first generation of English photographers. Hemphill's particular interests and beliefs added topics to the image agenda but he does not move outside it. Where he reconstructs the life of the working class in a tableau, he shows it in an idealised way. This idealisation by artists was common at that time [136].

Hemphill would appear to have been strongly influenced by contemporary art and culture in his topics. The Gulf of Spezzia was famous as the place where Shelley had died. His Biblical images may be derived from art being produced by the Pre-Raphaelites or from earlier art. Judith and Holofernes were common as a subject since Renaissance times as were still lives of plants and fruit. The imitation of fashionable painting styles was common in early photography, once they had moved on from simple recording. Hemphill would also appear to have been influenced by the art movement in photography in the 1850's in which combination printing from more than one negative was used. He has one print, *Judith with Holofernes' head. 1864* using this technique.

Upper-class society and culture at this time was strongly religious. Landscape and other scenic images were seen as having Christian significance. WDH was well aware of these given his and Mrs Osborne's commitment to a assertive Protestantism. He had been brought up during the Protestant revival of the 1820's. 'Biblical references still conditioned the idea of what was beautiful in nature', biblical scenes were common and even still lives of fruit had Christian associations[137]. Many of his photographs which today we would see as landscapes, still lives or nature studies, would have had a religious meaning for him.

At this time taking photographs of people meant that they had to pose carefully for several minutes to prevent blurring in the slow exposure time. WDH's early work sometimes shows a somewhat casual attitude to the placing of people in stereoscopic views. However the later larger prints show a meticulous care in the placing of people. The artillery officers and their wives are arranged about their gun. The group of people about Capt. Meecor, all women, are arranged around the central male figure, looking in various directions while he looks straight out. The posting of the artillery men beside their weapon, or firing from the bridge, are determined by military procedures. Big House groups are also carefully arranged, most again looking away from the camera. There are often single people posed in relation to, but not as important as an architectural monument. He often puts in a person to one side of a feature. In all his photographs he is concerned as to how the people in a photograph will become part of the larger image. Figures often appear in a landscape. They are sometimes ladies in full dress, but mostly gentlemen in top hats put in to give scale and stress the perspective. There are no figures in the fully interior views, probably due to the exposure length.

Biblical tableaux are posed with the people having somewhat wooden expressions. This is due to the exposure time but perhaps also to their lack of involvement in the creative act of arranging the photograph. There is a lack of emotion in photographs such as 'The Oat Field'. There are rare examples of people appearing, uncontrolled and animated, in his photographs. The crowd outside the 'Flower Show, Clonmel, April 1863' have definitely not been posed and have a casual vitality. The soldiers in 'Firing Royal Salute from New Bridge. Clonmel. Queen's Birthday. 1864' are in military, not photographic order. The people on Clonmel's quay in 'Quay thro' the arch of the Bridge - Clonmel' could not have been controlled from a distance and several are blurred.
Light and shade were very important to WDH. Several of his photographs have very dramatic areas of light and dark ('Interior. North Transept, Rock of Cashel. 1861.' for example). Variations of light and dark and the actual texture of carved stone work seemed to attract him. His landscapes are, at their best, broad vistas. WDH commonly put subjects seated or standing just inside a window, to take advantage of the strong side light. Most are looking away from the camera. Plants and trees are very common in his work as one would expect from his other interest. He often used trees or foliage to frame the image or a significant part of it. The girls in the Newtown Anner series of portraits are richly dressed with plants and flowers framing them. Favourite vases recur in photographs. Other props occur according to the topic of the photograph. The young 'Market Girl, Tipperary. 1863' is provided with a basket and an implausible tobacco pipe. 'Spezzia' and 'Rome' have flowers, statuettes and a spindle. The participants in 'Rebekah and Eliezer' are dressed in what was probably thought to be biblical dress and have pottery vessels and a rope for the well.

Chairs and tables recur in several images. Sometimes the table is used to support the subject's weight. An ornate chair with distinctive pattern from the Drawing Room, Newtown Anner is used in photographs taken over two years ('*The Opera Box*' and '*Miss Grace Osborne*'). A small table is used in two early photographs. A mirror, a cliché of early photography [138] is used in portraits of the Osborne girls. Ornate jewellery is worn by them. A bracelet reappears in several images. A jewellery box is visible on the table in one view. Many of the portraits show the girls and others doing something, spinning, playing the harp, painting, reading and gathering the harvest. Appropriate props are given so that we can identify the scene. In another photograph the prize cup he won is used as the basis of a still life. The books shown, where identifiable, are often his **Stereoscopic Illustrations** or linked with him. The doorway leading in from the conservatory was a favourite location, being well lit and comfortable. The small low balustrades which surrounded the pool can be seen in several views. Possessions, especially those of high artistic worth, were important to WDH.

His photographs are well focused, with a few exceptions. It is clear that at times he was very careful to have very sharp images, especially in his still lives ('*White Currants (The Prize of Prizes)*' for example). Some images appear to have been retouched ('*Miss Grace Osborne*') probably by the printer rather than WDH. Several of his images, possibly those he submitted to exhibitions and competitions are signed W.D. Hemphill in shaky and somewhat spiky letters. In one case the actual print edge cuts across the name, showing it was added to the negative. WDH worked with wet collodion negatives which had advantages over earlier methods. They allowed better defined detail, a greater range of tones and less exposure time. The process was however not easy to use, requiring in effect a portable darkroom to prepare and develop his images on site. The images in an album associated with Newtown Anner House were contact prints with a very wide range of exposure, up to half an hour in some cases. They were gold-toned after printing and some were retouched [139]. This would suggest to the author that they were printed by someone other than WDH, perhaps the firm who printed up his **Stereoscopic Illustrations**. We do not know if he moved to dry plate negatives which were available from 1880. He did note his use of Kodak film negatives on some photographs of the 1890's.

It is clear that WDH was well informed regarding contemporary techniques, exhibitions and advanced practitioners in London. He mentions photographic exhibitions, which he must have attended, in his lecture. Part of the local section of the 1858 Clonmel Art Exhibition was devoted to photographs. Most were shown by WDH: five were his own stereoscopic views and the rest were by well known British photographers, Caldesi and Montecchi, Spencer, Delamotte and Frith. Their subjects match his interests: the Royal Family and architectural views of Oxford, the interior of the Crystal Palace in London and views of the Holy Land. He also showed casts of the Elgin marbles from the temples of Minerva and Apollo while his wife and two young children exhibited items of artwork and jewellery. The other photographs shown were by Le Gray and Mayall. A supplement to the catalogue notes that John Bagwell exhibited Crimean photographs by Fenton and the Stereoscopic Company of London showed a set of stereographs and views[140]. All of this shows that Clonmel was not isolated from contemporary British photography. Even excluding attendance at exhibitions held elsewhere, in Dublin and across the Irish Sea, a wide variety of photographic work and art in general would have been locally accessible.

WDH's work fits into that by other photographers of the time. Historic architecture, bridges, artistic still lives and tableaux were all common. Some are very similar. Payne Jenning's views of *'The Old Weir Bridge, Killarney'* or *'Summer Scene On The Middle Lake Killarney'* are reminiscent of his work. Fenton's 1860 view of *The Terrace and Park at Harewood House* [141] is like WDH's view of the Geometric Garden at Newtown Anner (**Stereoscopic Illustrations**, image no. 60). Fenton's range of subjects [142], still lives, game, flowers and fruit, historical architecture is very similar to WDH's. WDH may have been influenced by him or by a common source. Even without arguing for this link (though works by Fenton were exhibited at the Clonmel Art exhibition of 1858) it is clear that WDH was in the mainstream of photographic development, but in the second wave. He would appear to have seen Lady Hawarden's work. While his photographs of the Newtown Anner girls have the same components[143] , they are less intense, with far less emotional charge between those photographer and subject. He may also have been familiar with Currey's work. We can presume that if he, for example, corresponded with Mr. Skaiffe he was familiar with the work of other Irish photographers.

WDH's familiarity with the work of English photographers was probably due not only to his attendance at exhibitions but also to his membership of the Amateur Photographic Association. This would be 'in keeping with his social and professional ambitions as most of the members were from the nobility and the gentry'[144] . The Amateur Photographic Association was founded in 1861 to promote the exchange of photographic art among members. It brought their work to the attention of a wider public through exhibitions and by circulation of pictures to subscribers. Membership of the APA carried a requirement to submit at least six negatives per year and entitled the member to receive two guineas' worth of prints[145] . Chandler notes that WDH was never a member of the Dublin Photographic Society, probably because he lived far from Dublin[146] .

WDH sent photographs to several major exhibitions and won fourteen prizes in Dublin, Paris and London[147] . He may have attended the London 1851 Exhibition and we must assume that he visited the photographic section of the 1853 Dublin Exhibition where he would have seen work by Continental, British and Irish practitioners[148] . A cutting of an article by S.C. Hall in The Art Journal fixed to the mount of *'Drawing Room Newtown Anner'* identifies it as ' *The work that was most prominent of the many of great excellence contributed by him* '(to the *Dublin International Exhibition of 1865)* [149] . A contemporary report notes that *'Dr. Hemphill, of Clonmel, also exhibits a variety of subjects, many of them pretty compositions and excellent photography'* [150]. Many other important photographers, including Lady Hawarden had work on show there.

'Most Gifted, Least Known', Contemporary and Later Comments

An advertising leaflet produced after the publication of **Stereoscopic Illustrations** quotes several favourable reviews [151]. The journal of the Photographic Society, London characterised the prints as *'admirable specimens of Photographic Art'*. The Art Journal thought the *'Photographic Pictures ... generally good, and many of them excellent'*. The Dublin Medical Press noted the perfection *'of workmanship and artistic taste'* and recommended that some of its readers should take up photography in preference to the *'rod, the gun or the hunting-whip'*. The Christian Examiner and the Clonmel Chronicle also praised both the photographs and the text while the then Kilkenny and South-East of Ireland Archaeological Society called it a magnificent volume. The Irish Builder of October 1st, 1860 said that *'we have never seen a work in all respects more exquisitely produced'* [152].

The cutting pasted to 'Drawing Room Newtown Anner' noted above also reads as follows *'Among Amateur Photographers, none rank higher than Dr. Hemphill, of Clonmel, who last year received the 1st prize at the Amateur Photographic Association, and this year has been awarded a medal at the Dublin International Exhibition. The work that was most prominent of the many of great excellence contributed by him, is the interior of a drawing-room, at Newton Armour (sic), the seat of R.B. Osborne, Esq. It is a production of surpassing skill, filled by a variety of graceful objects, each one of which comes out distinctly. As a triumph over more than the usual difficulties, it is perhaps the most remarkable effort of the Art'.*

Knowledge of Dr. Hemphill's photography seems to have died away in the first half of the 20th century. Photographic historians and, to a certain extent, local historians would have been aware of him. However his work would only have been available through the very rare copies of his book [153]. In the 1980's a number of articles containing reproductions of his work appeared, some apparently prompted by the active interest shown by his descendants. Some articles appeared in newspapers and popular magazines [154]. A discussion of the railway engine shown at Clonmel Railway station in **Stereoscopic Illustrations** was also published in 1985 [155]. O'Connell in his survey of Irish photography, describes WDH as an enthusiastic amateur and reproduces his image of in *'Quay thro' the arch of the Bridge - Clonmel'* showing the Gashouse Bridge over the River Suir with barges alongside the quay and two men working on the gas light on the bridge [156]. Sexton has a copy of *'Lady Blessington's Bath'*, described as an albumen print from a wet plate negative, c 1865 and a 'gold-toned albumen' image, perhaps one of a stereoscopic pair, of two milk maids in a farmyard with a haystack behind [157]. Dodier in her description of Clementina, Lady Hawarden 's photographic career, mentions WDH as a fellow amateur, noting that Dundrum House did not figure among his subjects or the Hawardens among his dedicatees. She goes on to say that from about 1864 he began to photograph tableaux of Mrs Osborne's daughters at Newtown Anner in a style that reminded viewers of her work [158].

Several authors have used his images to illustrate books describing the Irish Big House. Mark Bence-Jones used WDH's view of the Drawing Room, his portrait of Grace and a small view of the two sisters at the Temple in his chapter about the house and its family [159]. Girouard in his evocative description of the house and its people also reproduces several Hemphill views [160] and describes Dr. Hemphill as a 'surgeon, grower of orchids, collector of Waterford glass, skilled ivory-turner and one of the most gifted, least known of early photographers'. Scarry has published the Brunskill album containing four Hemphill photographs. Chandler noted WDH as the 'most ambitious of the early Irish amateur stereoscopic photographers' [161]. More recently his photographs have been used to illustrate several local historical works such as O'Donnell's history of Clonmel [162]. Copies of his images held by the Irish Architectural Archive have also illustrated descriptions of buildings such as Mitchelstown Castle[163] . Chandler in his recent survey of Irish photography again discusses WDH's work and **Stereoscopic Illustrations** noting that that WDH was one of the 'most famous photographers of the day' [164].

Conclusions

Hardly known for many years, at his best Dr. W. D. Hemphill's photographic images are simply superb works of art. This doctor in a small Irish county town produced beautiful images which are the result of much determination and preparation. We do not know where he received his art education, whether informal or formal, or his photographic training. It is clear however that he was a Renaissance man, gifted in art, craft, music and scientific investigation. His photographs are a testimony to his skills but also, more importantly (especially to himself), to his beliefs, religious, political and social. Within twenty years of his death, the world he knew and in which he had a prominent position had vanished. Dr. Hemphill's photography not only preserved 'a record of the many beautiful and in some cases little known localities in the neighbourhood' as he intended but also is a record of the Big House, its society in South Tipperary and the life and interests of one of its members. In today's fast changing South Tipperary such records are invaluable, all the more so when they are so beautiful.

Text Illustrations:

Plates

These illustrations are those originally selected for a special travelling exhibition of reproductions of Dr. Hemphill's work. They are a small portion of the known output but are a representative sample.

Original titles, printed in italics, are quoted directly when possible and were mostly obtained from an album which appears to be his own collection of his work. Those prints reproduced from the Newtown Anner album in private possession have less information but there are later identifications in pencil of some of the scenes. Dates can be established from other sources in some cases. The titles of the stereoscopic photographs were taken from **Stereoscopic Illustrations.**

'Round Tower, Rock of Cashel 1857 45 sec'

This photograph was obviously important to WDH as he used it as the first and only large size photograph in his book, **Stereoscopic Illustrations** . It shows two of his interests, archaeology and photography. The figure standing somewhat self-consciously, beside the camera is probably WDH himself. It has been suggested that he is posing as if timing an exposure, watch in hand. There must have been another camera and perhaps a photographer there as well. The ruins in the background are so well known as to be a symbol of Tipperary and Ireland throughout the world. The Round Tower was build after the Rock of Cashel, a royal fortress, was handed over to the Church in 1101. The present cathedral behind the tower dates to the thirteenth century. After an eventful history, which included two burnings, the cathedral on the Rock was abandoned in 1749. The site is now Ireland's premier National Monument with thousands of visitors each year.

EC Album 1, image 23. Titled as 'Cloictheach on the Rock of Cashel' in **Stereoscopic Illustrations**

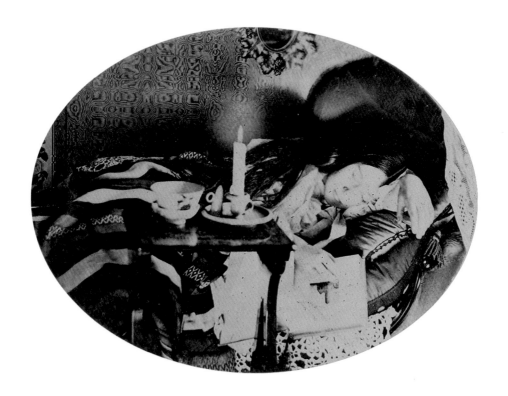

W. D. Hemphill's Daughter?

While this photograph is posed and the various 'props' carefully arranged, there is a feeling of tenderness and affection for this girl. She is shown passive and innocent, rather than active and self-controlled. This print is both undated and untitled but the book seems to be open at a view of the Rock of Cashel taken by WDH. If it is Howitt's **Ruined Abbeys and Castles of Great Britain and Ireland**, published in 1864, then this photograph must be from that year or later. The photograph used in the book would date to between 1857 and 1864. In 1864 Hemphill's daughter, May, was aged eleven and so it may be her. The subject is likely to be a close relative, as few of his photographs are so intimate.

EC Album 1, image 113.

'*S.W. Hemphill, 1864, 7 Sects*'

WDH must have been proud of Samuel, his son's musical skills. He himself was a noted musician. This portrait was taken in 1864 when Samuel was 13. Samuel seems to have followed the family tradition of entering the medical profession. In later years he and his father quarrelled when Samuel married someone whom his father did not approve of. Samuel's daughter, Eva, eventually inherited Oak Ville, the family home in Clonmel.

EC Album 1, image 48.

H.B.Pedder, 7th Hussars, 1862, 20 Sects'

WDH married Sarah Pedder who came from a prominent Clonmel family. This portrait is of H.B. Pedder who seems to have been W. D. Hemphill's brother-in-law. He is wearing the uniform of the Hussars, a cavalry regiment of the British Army. The ornate uniform with its lace, sword, sash and fur cap must have been a special point of interest for the photographer. A copy of this photograph hung in the Drawing Room of the Hemphill family home in Brighton Place, Clonmel. Henry Pedder started his military career as an Ensign with the Tipperary Artillery Militia in 1854, transferring as a Captain to the 4th Light Dragoons in 1861 [166].

EC Album 1, image 37.

'St. Mary's Church, North'

St. Mary's was built as the parish church of Clonmel in the 13th century and is now the Church of Ireland parish church. St. Mary's was WDH's church and he was devoted to it and to the Church of Ireland. He photographed St. Mary's several times during his life as prints dating from 1857, 1862 and the early 1890's survive. It has had many alterations, especially in 1805 and 1857. This early photograph is one of several taken by WDH to record the church before the alterations of 1857. Among the changes were the removal of the stepped battlements and the raising of the roof. The photographs are not of the same artistic standard as WDH reached several years later but are important as a record of the church. They may have been taken in the winter or early spring as there are no leaves on the trees. WDH had a set of prints bound up in a small private album which he presented to the 'Rev. Richard Hemphill from his affect. Brother WDH Clonmel July 22nd 1857'. In recent years the church has again been renovated, with the late Col. S. J. Watson playing a major part in the raising of funds for the work.

Ex.343.3

'Rebekah and Eliezer. 1864. 4 Seconds'

The setting up of groups showing scenes from literature was common in early photography. This Biblical scene, *'Rebekah and Eliezer'*, is evidence of WDH's strong Christian faith. However a close look at it hints that the girls acting in it are not enjoying it very much. They seem, or are made to seem submissive as only one is looking directly at the photographer. The location and 'props' have been chosen to suggest a well at which the girls have been drawing water. Even allowing for the need to remain still, the girls have very wooden, even bored expressions. It is likely that Dr. Hemphill's interest in the story he was portraying was at least as strong as his interest in the people he used to show it.

The people in the photograph or the location must have some significant link with Newtown Anner. The man is probably H.B. Pedder and the four girls are obviously related to each other. They appear in other Newtown Anner photographs. It is possible that they are his sisters, Sarah (married WDH in 1849), Ruth, Alice Mary and Helen Elizabeth. The Pedders were visitors to the Osbornes but each of the girls seems too young to be Sarah. Four Quin sisters known to the Osbornes are mentioned in a Valentine sent to Grace Osborne in 1864 and now in a scrapbook of hers in Hatfield House. They lived at Rochestown House, near Cahir, and were part of Big House artistic circles [167].

EC Album 1, image 66

The Library, Oakville, 1892'

You can tell a lot from a person's workshop or study especially when he is sufficiently proud of it and the qualities it represents to photograph it. Here is the evidence of W. D. Hemphill's interests and hobbies: his billiards table, his piano, sheet music and busts of composers, his geological cabinet, lined with specimens, and his microscope. The bookcase is lined with journals and books and the walls are covered with prints and photographs, some of antiquarian subjects and one possibly his own. His obituary noted that *'His rooms were filled with beautiful photographic views'*. There are several ivory turnings, probably his own, and other knick-knacks and dust catchers on the shelves.

EC Album 3, image 17.

'Orchid House W.D.H. 1860 25 Minutes APA'

Orchid growing requires a great deal of patience and dedication. In the last century it was fashionable for well–to-do people to grow them and other hothouse plants. William D. Hemphill had a green-house and a hot-house at his own house, Oak Ville in Clonmel and this photograph may have been taken there. However he did not buy Oak Ville until 1871 though he may have rented it before then. The small balustrade on the right appears in several of his images, including those of the Osborne sisters and so the Orchid House was probably at Newtown Anner. This photograph is the result of a very long exposure time. The letters A. P. A. refer to his membership of the Amateur Photographic Association, which was established in 1859. Its members could order prints from negatives contributed by other members. The earliest photographic clubs swapped photographs among their members. By 1859 commercialism was beginning to appear, as photography became much more common. The members of the A.P.A. paid for their prints.

EC Album 1, image 55.

'Autumn & Summer Fruit 1864 2 Minutes'

The early photographers inherited traditional subjects from earlier artists. These still lives are beautiful works of art in the same way as a painted picture. They do have other meanings however. Only the well-off would have had access to expensive fruits such as these and to the fine china and glass items. WDH collected Waterford crystal glass. The photographs would also have been intended to show the photographer's ability to record the different textures and details. Like all photographs therefore they tell us as much about the photographer as the image recorded. The title for this photograph in a family album identifies it as a 'Wothlytype'. This printing process used a paper coated with collodion containing uranium and silver nitrate. It was invented by J. Wothly of Aachen in 1864 but did not survive more than a couple of years. WDH, or his photographic printer, was familiar with contemporary technical techniques.

1993.269.35 (copied from Newtown Anner album in private possession).

'Flower Show, Clonmel, April 1863, half secd'

In January, 1854 WDH was one of three Trustees of the County of Tipperary Horticultural Society who leased a plot of land from John Bagwell to the north of the present Queen Street in Clonmel to add to their existing Horticultural Garden. This photograph shows the Flower Show there in April, 1863. A military band is playing under the marquee. A small crowd is at the entrance as people arrive by carriage and trap. Is that the Fever Hospital and Prior Park Terrace in the background? W. D. Hemphill seems to have taken this photograph from his house in Brighton Place and looking down the present-day Queen Street. The Garden would seem to have been where the present Rink Garage is today.

EC Album 1, image 17b.

White Currants, 1 Minute, Prize A.P.A. 1867 Paris Exhibition'

WDH won a number of prizes for his photography at international exhibitions in London, Dublin and Paris as well as from the Amateur Photographic Association and the London Photographic Society. In 1865 he won the prize of a silver cup from the Amateur Photographic Association. This photograph is dated 1867 and shows the prize cup (the date on the cup is 1865 though a mark makes it seem as if it is 1885). It seems to be the photograph which won a prize from the A.P.A. and a Certificate of Honour at the International Exhibition in Paris in 1867. A copy in an A.P.A. album in the Royal Photographic Society, Bath is titled 'White Currants (Prize of Prizes)'. WDH returned to this topic at least once more.

EC Album 1, image 97.

'Rock of Cashel, South East. 1861 30 secs. A.P.A.
Hon. Mention Gt. Exhibition 1862'

Ruined churches and abbeys were standard subjects for landscape painters in the late eighteenth and early nineteenth centuries. The early photographers followed this by photographing sites like the Rock of Cashel. They were attracted by tradition and the character of the country rather than, for example, new buildings or industry.

EC Album 1, image 27. Signed

'Interior. North Transept, Rock of Cashel. 1861. 3 Minutes.
Hon. Mention Gt. Exhib. 1862'

This carefully posed photograph took three minutes to take during which the two gentlemen had to keep absolutely still to prevent the image blurring. WDH signed it at the bottom left, probably when he sent it to the Great Exhibition of 1862 in London where he won an 'Honourable Mention'. Here he seems to be interested in the play of light and shadow in the central part of the cathedral, under the tower. The two gentlemen are carefully placed in the light. A romantic love of ruins underlies the idea to take this photograph. He had previously taken it as a stereoscopic photographic pair for his book but that view has less light and the viewpoint is not as well placed. WDH seems to have often returned to take a second and better view of a particular location.

EC Album 1, image 21.

'Flamboyant Window St. Dominic's Abbey, Cashel 1861 2 minutes A.P.A.
Hon: Mention Gt. Exhibition 1862'

At the time WDH took this photograph, photography was dominated by certain themes. Some subjects seemed natural things to photograph and many were derived from painting. The earliest photographers, active in the 1840's, made pictures that reflected their social class and interests. The study of ancient monuments was one of these interests. By the 1860's advances in the quality of negatives and prints meant that exact detail and clarity were seen as desirable in a photograph. Here WDH seems to be attracted to the textures of the various pieces of stonework. The Dominician Friary in Cashel was founded in 1242 and was restored after a fire in 1480. The earlier plain windows were replaced by ornate windows, one of which is seen here.

EC Album 1, image 26.

'Holycross Abbey, 1863. Dry Plate 7 secs'

Holycross Abbey, a Cistercian monastery sited beside the River Suir, was founded in 1169 and takes its name from the relic of the True Cross which was preserved there in medieval times. The Abbey continued in use into the 17th century but then fell into ruins. It was extensively restored in 1971-5 and is now in use as the parish church.

EC Album 1, image 17a.

'Cahir Castle, East 1861. 30 seconds'

Cahir castle was founded by the Normans in the 13th century. It was granted to the Butler family who continued their connection with it until modern times. The castle was captured in 1599 by the Earl of Essex, in 1647 by Lord Inchiquin and in 1650 by Oliver Cromwell. Richard Butler, Earl of Glengall, landlord of Cahir and the surrounding area, restored the castle between 1840 and 1846. His architect, William Tinsley also redesigned much of the town square. The costs eventually bankrupted the estate but the Earl's daughter later bought back most of it. Her son, Lieut. Col. Richard Butler Charteris, was the last Butler to hold the castle which is now a National Monument

This view is taken from the east, from the area of the present Allied Irish Bank. Today this area is part of the car park and the river here is much narrower. The ladies on the left probably came with WDH. The carts in the river may be being washed out or perhaps their wheels are being dampened to keep the wood from shrinking and loosening.

EC Album 1, image 7.

'St. Patrick's Well'

St. Patrick's Well, near Marlfield village, is believed to have been visited by St. Patrick. At the well are the ruins of a small church and a simple cross. In the past the well was a popular place of pilgrimage. It has been altered and tidied up several times since this photograph was taken in the summers of 1857-8. The tree which used to stand beside the well is long gone and there is no longer an old lady who sells souvenirs as there was then. The waters of the well now flow into a wide shallow pool. The well is still a popular excursion spot for Clonmel people.

From a stereoscopic print pair, **Stereoscopic Illustrations**, no. Liv 1857/8

'*Ardfinnan Castle*'

Ardfinnan Castle still stands overlooking the River Suir though it is now covered with ivy and the trees have grown up around it. A thirteenth century round tower and a square tower overlooking the river are the main features. The castle was attacked and captured by the Cromwellians. The buildings lower down, beside the river, are probably part of the Woollen Mill which closed in living memory

From a stereoscopic print pair, **Stereoscopic Illustrations**, no. xxxvi, 1857/8.

Clonmel in W. D. Hemphill's time.

In WDH's time, as today, Clonmel was the administrative centre for South Tipperary. Local government, the courts, army, police and the prison system all had branches if not headquarters here. When he returned to Clonmel to join his father's practice and settle down, the town was a prosperous market town. In 1841 it had a population of over 13,000 people, making it the second biggest inland town in the country. By the time he was an old man, in the 1880's, Clonmel's population had been reduced by nearly one third. The huge corn milling industry, with over twenty mills in the Clonmel area, was in decline. Farmers and industrialists turned to livestock farming and industries such as bacon curing and tanning. Employment declined overall. Towns such as Thurles benefited and Clonmel suffered as the new railways reduced the importance of goods transport on the river Suir. Dr. Hemphill caught some of these changes in his photographs: the barges still on the river but a train at the new railway station, the Bianconi long car also to be made redundant by the railways and the administrative buildings and people such as the Lunatic Asylum and the soldiers from the barracks.

'District Lunatic Asylum, Clonmel *1863 12 secs*'

State care in Ireland for the mentally ill began in 1814 when the first of several asylums were built. Clonmel Lunatic Asylum, as it was called, was built in 1834. Then, as now, providing work for the patients to do as therapy was often thought worthwhile. Here some of the male patients seem to be working in the garden. There are several attendants and perhaps some of the medical staff. One of the patients seems to have been a soldier as he is standing to attention with his spade as if it were a rifle. WDH was Consulting Physician to the Clonmel District and Auxiliary Asylums. This important position meant that he was responsible for the patients' physical condition and also decided if they were well enough to be discharged. His links with the Asylum explain the photograph and he may have been connected in some way with the work the patients are seen doing in it. Today St. Luke's looks very similar except that the high wall that used to surround it has been gone for many years.

EC Album 1, image 88.

'Scots' Church, Anglesea street –Clonmel'

It would be very foolish to stand in Anglesea Street today to take a photograph. It is a busy street with a constant stream of cars driving down towards the Quays. The buildings in the street look very similar though the railings outside the Scots Church are now gone. The mountain has become overgrown since the photograph was taken in 1857/8. The Scots Church was built in 1838 by a group of Unitarians. It was sold in 1970. The houses along the street were built about the same time.

Take a close look at the vehicle left in the street. It is probably a Bianconi long car, perhaps of the type known as the 'Faugh a Bealach' (Get out of the way!). By the late 1850's Bianconi's business was under severe pressure from the railways. The first train came into Clonmel in April 1852. The headquarters of Bianconi's transport network was in Parnell Street nearby.

From a stereoscopic print pair, **Stereoscopic Illustrations**, no. xlix.

'Railway Station, Clonmel'

This photograph, taken in 1857 or 1858, is believed to be the earliest one from Ireland of a railway engine and train. The railway station in Clonmel was built in 1852. This seems to be the 5.15 p.m. train from Waterford, due out of Clonmel at 6.50. The steam engine was one of six built for the Waterford and Limerick Railway. In 1867 this train carried both passengers and goods. The engine seems to be moving some goods wagons after filling up with water from the column on the right.

From a stereoscopic print pair, **Stereoscopic Illustrations**, no. Li.

'Firing Royal Salute from New Bridge. Clonmel. Queen's Birthday. 1864
1/4 second A.P.A.'

In 1864, Queen Victoria had reigned for twenty-seven years. The British Empire was one of the world powers. Ireland was part of that empire and dates like the Queen's birthday were marked by public events. Here the artillery from the Clonmel barracks are firing a salute to mark the Queen's birthday. WDH took several photographs of the soldiers and officers in Clonmel. The officers would have been part of the town's middle class and he obviously knew them. Most towns in Ireland had an army barracks as their function would have been to control the country. This network of barracks has been inherited by us today and some commentators believe that we have too many but, as Clonmel knows well, towns will fight to retain their own. The Gas House bridge would have been comparatively new when this photograph was taken as it was built in the first half of the nineteenth century, along with the Presentation Convent Bridge, when the Old Bridge in the town could not accommodate the growing traffic.

The guns being fired are Armstrong guns, first adopted by the British artillery in 1858. Although technically a great advance on the muzzle-loading guns used up to then, they were criticised as 'terribly complicated' by an officer corps chosen for their qualities as gentlemen rather than technical ability. In 1864 the British Government stopped the manufacture of Armstrong guns and reverted to the old style guns for fifteen years. WDH may have been conscious of the technical innovation as there is a photograph of one being loaded among the several images of the artillery officers, men and their guns. He may have heard the officers discussing them.

EC Album 1, image 52.

'Lady Blessington's Bath, Prize Silver Cup. 1866. 7 secs.'

This part of the River Suir in Clonmel is linked with Marguerite Power (1789-1849) who became a well-known writer in her later years, after two marriages, the first being arranged by her father when she was fifteen. She is supposed to have bathed here when living in Clonmel as a child. The quiet pool is formed by a weir erected to collect sufficient water to power the mills that were common in Clonmel. There is a long tradition in Clonmel of boating on the Suir. The Clonmel Rowing Club was founded in 1869 but this photograph shows that there may have been an earlier club. It is likely that this particular oarsman and his passenger are middle class as they are well dressed. He seems to be wearing an ornate cap of the type used in sport then. They were often given as a presentation and the idea survives with the phrase 'He was capped for Ireland'. Note the flag on the boat. It seems to be the British Union Flag. This would also suggest that the oarsman and his companion were part of the town's establishment, many of whom would have been Unionist [168].

EC Album 1, image 89.

'Clonmel from Merlin, Sepr. 1862 Dry Plate 90 seconds APA'

We can see the Gas House Bridge through the trees. It was called that because the Clonmel Gas Works used to be on the far end of the bridge, where a large block of apartments has been built. Beyond the bridge we can see the houses along the quay and the town. The photograph was taken from the upper part of Merlin, a house along the Coleville road. The house is still there and the small monkey-puzzle tree in the garden is now very tall.

EC Album 1, image 1.

'Ashbourne Clonmel. 1863. A.P.A. 30 seconds'

Ashbourne, a house on the Waterford side of the River Suir, at the end of the Gas House bridge, was built by William Tinsley, the Clonmel architect for Robert Davis. The Coleville road suburb of Clonmel was developed in the mid-1800's as a area of houses for prosperous business and professional families. This photograph is very carefully posed with the position of each person being deliberately chosen. WDH was an admirer of art and would have seen prints and paintings of scenes like this. They would have inspired him to try to arrange his own photographs. The exterior of the house has changed very little today.

EC Album 1, image 4.

'Quay thro' the arch of the Bridge- Clonmel'

Today we use the River Suir for enjoyment. We walk by it, row on it, fish and swim in it. In the past it was also an important transport route. Once a heavy cargo was loaded on a boat it could be moved long distances much easier than on the rough untarred roads. A towpath was built along the river and the bollards on the Quays show the marks of the ropes used to tie up the boats. Commercial barges, like the ones in the photograph, were used less after the Waterford to Limerick railway was finished in 1854. The river traffic ended in the early 1920's . This photograph has a carefully chosen viewpoint and was probably posed. It is taken beside the Gas House Bridge. Beyond the barges we can see the quays of Clonmel, built for the river trade when the town wall along the river was demolished in the late eighteenth century. Some of the buildings along the Quay, such as the 'Boot Factory' (now Government Offices) are still there but the Manor Mills in the background have been demolished. The man on the ladder is working on the gas light. Gas lighting was introduced into Clonmel in 1824[169] .

From a stereoscopic print pair, **Stereoscopic Illustrations,** no. xlvi, 1857-8.

'Two Mile Bridge, River Anner 1863. Dry Plate 5 minutes A.P.A.'

The River Anner flows into the Suir a few miles to the east of Clonmel. The Clonmel to Waterford road crosses the Anner at Two Mile Bridge. WDH would have passed over this bridge on his way to visit the Osborne family at Newtown Anner. Trees and bridges were favourite topics of the early photographers.

EC Album 1, image 18.

'Drawing Room. Newtown Anner 30 minutes
1st prize picture Gold Medal. Amateur Photographic Association 1864.
Prize Medal (specially mentioned) International Exhibition. Dublin 1865'

WDH won prizes for this photograph in 1864 and 1865. By then photographers thought that clarity and detail were important rather than the artistry and impressions of the earliest amateurs. The room was redecorated sometime in the 1850's, either by Lady Osborne or by her daughter, Catherine Bernal Osborne. It was 'repapered, using a diaper design with a scrolled border and fitted up with an Aubusson carpet, a Venetian chandelier, and pelmets, overmantle, mirror and brass and steel grate with matching furniture, all in the Victorian Rococo style[170]'. Most of the paintings were from the Bernal collection, a fabulous collection of works of art made by Catherine's father-in-law, Ralph Bernal and auctioned off in thirty-two days in 1854 for the then colossal sum of £71,000.

WDH was taking photographs at Newtown Anner in the mid-1850's and continued into the 1860's. Presumably he continued to visit, at least until the Bernal Osbornes died in the 1880's though there does not appear to be photographs into the 1870's.

EC Album 1, image 33.

'The Geometric-Garden, Newtown Anner'

It is likely that this garden was built by Lady Osborne who spent much of her time redesigning the gardens at Newtown Anner. She had married her 58-year-old husband when she was only aged nineteen or twenty and lived a lonely life due to his antisocial tendencies. This is one of a pair of stereoscopic photographs taken in the summer of 1857 or 1858 and used in Hemphill's book.

From a stereoscopic print pair, **Stereoscopic Illustrations**, no. lxi .

'View from Dining room, Newtown Anner, A.P.A. 1864 8 seconds'.

In 1830 Edwin Budding invented the first lawn mower "for the purpose of cropping and shearing the vegetable surface of lawns"[171] . Mowing the lawn is still a chore to be done but in 1864 it required two men, two women and a horse to pull the mower. Today the petrol engine and the cost of labour means that most of us have the pleasure of doing it ourselves. The girl in the front is probably either Edith or Grace Osborne, with her mother perhaps. The hill in the background is the famed Slievenamon. This view has been published by Girouard[172].

EC Album 1, image 71.

'The Temple - Newtown Anner'

WDH wrote in **Stereoscopic Illustration**s that in 1846 Lady Osborne, wishing to help the local people *'employed a large number of the starving peasantry in cutting down unsightly hills and elevations, filling stagnant ponds, or converting them into beautiful canals and sheets of water, making walks and terraces, and succeeding in converting one of the most uninteresting portions of the demesne into as lovely and enjoyable a spot as the eye could rest on'. 'From the upper terrace walks, flights of stone steps, some of them ornamented with sculpture, lead downwards to the water, which consists of formal-shaped canals and ponds, harmonising well with the general character of the artificial scenery of this part of the demesne. At the extreme west, on a raised mound planted with evergreens, stands a little summer-house, in the form of an ancient Greek temple, with Doric portico, extremely elegant in design'.* A letter by Lady Osborne in Bath, dated April 13th, 1850[173] notes that she *'went to see a famous iron shop, and there I made two purchases, … the other a small beautiful round table for the temple for two guineas. ….I think the table for the temple is a nice thing to have for reading and writing when we sit there, which I shall so often do in the summer…'.* The ponds and canals are still there and hold some water but not as much as in the past due to modern drainage works. The temple is in ruins but the present owner of the house is restoring all.

From a stereoscopic print pair, **Stereoscopic Illustrations**, no. Lviii

'The Slope. Newtown Anner, 1862. Dry Plate. 4 minutes A.P.A.'

This beautiful photograph is one of WDH's best and shows both his strengths and weaknesses as a photographer. He clearly had a deep knowledge of art and wanted to create works of art. Here he has managed to capture the stillness and beauty of a length of water that mirrors the scenery. The persons are carefully posed to provide interest. We wonder who they are and why are they on opposite sides of the canal? The old trees emphasise the history and interest of the place. However, for all its beauty, the photograph has little life in it and the people are figures in the landscape. Dr. Hemphill's photographs only become personal when he is recording his close family. He took at least two other versions of this view with different groupings of people.

1993.269.18 (copied from Newtown Anner album in private possession)

'*Miss Grace Osborne. 1864. 12 seconds*'

Grace Osborne of Newtown Anner was seventeen when this photograph was taken. She and her sister, Edith, were noted for their cleverness, beautiful hands and attractive voices. Grace inherited Newtown Anner and married the Duke of St. Albans. She lived for many years as a widow and died in 1926. The house descended through her husband's family until it was sold and its contents removed in 1987. Its present owner is now restoring it.

EC Album 1, image 45.

'Portrait. Evening. 1866 2 minutes'

A portrait of a young woman reflected in a mirror was a common subject for the early photographers. It allowed the photographer to show two views of the person and to use the available light to the best advantage. It also allowed the photographer, and the viewer, to see a private moment, a young woman checking her image in the mirror. This photograph was taken in 1866 and is probably of Grace Osborne dressed for dinner. It was taken in the Drawing Room of Newtown Anner.

EC Album 1, image 92.

'Roman Girl. 1863. 25 sec's. A.P.A.'

Charades and dressing up were part of how the young people of the Big Houses amused themselves. The early photographers also sometimes liked to recreate paintings, stories and emotions in their images. Here Edith Osborne is dressed up as an Italian country girl (or what they thought an Italian girl would look like). There may be a private family joke here as she was known for her dark complexion. It was said that she had inherited them from her father's Spanish Jewish ancestors.

EC Album 1, image 45, also copied (1993.269.12) from the Newtown Anner album in private possession.

The Artist. 15 secs, 1866'

Both of the Osborne sisters, Grace and Edith, were talented artists. Their mother, Catherine Osborne, invited artists to stay at Newtown Anner so that they could learn from them. In 1866, Edith would have been 21 years of age and this could be her [174]. The artist is painting what seems to be a religious scene in oils with a large portrait in the background. Art was one of the acceptable pastimes for young ladies. Edith Osborne married Henry Arthur Blake, a police officer from Galway who was disliked by her parents because of his lack of a fortune. However he had a very successful career, and was appointed Governor of several colonies. She continued her painting until her old age and is noted for her accurate paintings of plants and insects.

EC Album 1, image 94.

'Market Girl, Tipperary. 1863. 20 seconds A.P.A.'

It is said that the camera never lies but, of course, it can be made to. Here we have a portrait of a young country girl going to market. But look closer. Her shoes (and she has them) are clean. Her hair is clean and well combed. The basket and pipe are arranged about her. Her expression shows she is part of a charade, not a real market girl imposed upon. This is probably Grace Osborne who was sixteen years of age in 1863. It was common for Big House people to dress up like the people who worked for them for photographs.

EC Album 1, image 47.

'The Oatfield. 1864. 7 seconds'

Yet again the camera never lies or can it? Is this a group of farm workers at the harvest? No, it is not. They look away from the camera either because they are acting a scene or because they really would prefer not to be involved. These are the girls who posed in 'Rebekah and Eliezer'. They may be related to Dr. Hemphill's wife, Sarah Pedder as her brother is in 'Rebekah and Eliezer' as well. This photograph was taken on the Newtown Anner estate with Slievenamon in the background. Finally have you noticed the real farm workers on the right, behind the girls?

EC Album 1, image 66 and copied (1993.269.4) from Newtown Anner album in private possession.

'Our First Drawing Room. 40 seconds. 1867.'

These two very confident young women are formally dressed. The title of the photograph and perhaps their attitude suggests that they were reconstructing and recording their first formal event in Dublin at which they were introduced to the Lord Lieutenant and polite society. Young women of the land-owning classes would have been very restricted in what they could do. Art and music were acceptable pastimes but there was a fear of being left unmarried and a spinster. It was very important therefore to be introduced to society and eligible bachelors. It was important also to dress fashionably even if that meant having your waist crushed artificially and painfully to achieve the required feminine profile.

The distinctive decorative motif of a continuous running scroll under the window sill has been identified [175] as being in the Saloon, Castletown Cox, Co. Kilkenny. These two girls could be Geraldine and Evelyn, daughters of Katherine Cox, sister and heir to Sir Richard Cox, the last male Cox of Castletown, and her husband, Col. William Villiers-Stuart, M.P. for Waterford. They were married in 1833 and had three daughters and two sons of whom Geraldine and Evelyn were the last born. Geraldine married in 1874 (Burke 1904). A second photograph, of the same girls and two other older women, *'The Harpist 1867',* was possibly taken in the garden front arcade at the house.

EC Album 1, image 84.

'Castletown 1867'

Castletown Cox is situated to the north of Carrick-on Suir, a few miles away from Clonmel. It has been described as one of the loveliest country houses in Ireland. It was begun in 1767 and was built for the Archbishop of Cashel. In 1867 it was owned by the Villiers-Stuart family of Dromana , one of whom had married a Cox heiress. It is likely that some of the family are included in this photograph. Perhaps they had invited friends to come and play croquet, a sport suitable for mixed company?

In 1785 Dorothea Herbert recorded that a previous generation of *The Coxes were figuring away every Winter in Dublin universally admired for their Beauty and Hauton for they spared No Expence on their appearance- to the tune of 8000 a year and a vast accumulated Debt while fifty Servants in Livery Graced their train besides others of all Ranks'[176] . The house has survived well and is being restored by its present owner.

EC Album 1, image 99.

'Drawing Room, Marlfield 1865. 25 minutes'

Marlfield House and the pretty village about it are a short distance to the west of Clonmel. The Bagwell family lived at Marlfield from the late 1700's until the 1980's. It is possible that some or all of the furniture and paintings seen here did not survive the burning of the house by Anti-Treaty forces on the 9th of January, 1923. They did so as part of the policy of reprisals against those Anglo-Irish landowners who had taken seats in the new Free State Senate. The house was re-built and has now been converted into apartments. This photograph was probably taken not as a historical record by WDH but as a tribute to the good taste of the house's owners. WDH and his contemporaries in society valued fine works of art and furniture.

EC Album 1, image 61.

Kilmanahan Castle

Kilmanahan Castle, now ruined, consists of a late Georgian house added to an earlier castle. It overlooks the river Suir a short distance to the south-west of Clonmel. The Greene family lived there from the seventeenth century until the cost of the conversion of 'a Georgian house with medieval tower into a neo-Gothic castle', £20,000, ruined the family [177]. Later on, like Knocklofty House across the river, it was owned by the Earls of Donoughmore. This view was probably taken in the mid-1860's as a view of the house from another angle is labelled 'Silver Cup Amateur Photographic Association 1865 '[178].

Copied (1993.269.26) from Newtown Anner album in private possession.

'Shanbally Castle and Porch'

Shanbally Castle was built for the O'Callaghan family, Viscounts Lismore, in 1812 and replaced an earlier house. The family originally came from County Cork. The demesne around the house was then over 1200 acres in size. It remained in the family until 1954 when the estate of 750 arable and 250 wooded acres was acquired by the Land Commission. In 1960, despite efforts to save it, the castle was demolished because no buyer could be found. Its demolition has been called 'one of Ireland's great architectural losses this century'. The house was designed by Nash at a cost of £90,000 and had twenty main bedrooms and sitting rooms, marble fireplaces and mahogany staircases and doors. It was used by the I.R.A. during the Truce and by the Army during the Second World War. Only the overgrown and rubble filled basements now remain.

From a stereoscopic print pair, Stereoscopic Illustrations, no.lxxviii.

'*Gurteen. 20 secs. 1866*'

W. D. Hemphill photographed Gurteen near Kilsheelan, to the east of Clonmel, in 1866, the same year as the house was built for the de la Poer family. They were very friendly with the Osbornes of Newtown Anner. The house has survived and the land around it is still owned by the family.

EC Album 1, image 98.

'Lismore Castle, North'

Lismore has had important buildings since Early Christian times when there was a famous monastery there. The present castle, seen here in WDH's stereograph of 1857/8, mostly dates from the nineteenth centuries with some earlier parts. Richard Boyle, an Elizabethan adventurer, came to Ireland with little, eventually became the very rich Earl of Cork and bought the castle and its lands from Sir Walter Raleigh. The castle passed to the Dukes of Devonshire by marriage in 1748 and they still own it. The gardens are open to the public.

From a stereoscopic print pair, Stereoscopic Illustrations, no. xxv.

'*Anner Castle*'

Anner castle is on the east bank of the river Anner, north east of Clonmel. It belonged to the Mandeville family and incorporated their old family castle, Ballinahy castle. It was burnt in a fire in 1926 and only the front part was rebuilt.

From a stereoscopic print pair, **Stereoscopic Illustrations**, no. lxxix.

'Mitchelstown Castle, East'

Mitchelstown castle was built in 1823-5 and has been described as the 'the largest and most successful of the earlier Gothic Revival castles'[180]. It had 60 bedrooms and sometimes as many as one hundred people staying there. In 1842 a visitor noted that the glass houses were 488 feet long and the conservatory 100 feet by 40. A German visitor called the castle 'a huge heap of stone which has cost its possessor £50,000'[181]. Big George, 3rd Earl of Kingston, was the builder of the castle. His family had inherited the lands through marriage from the extinct FitzGerald White Knights. He went mad in 1832 when his tenants dared to vote against his chosen candidate in a by-election. His successors continued to live lavishly. The bailiffs arrived in 1844 but had to besiege the castle for a fortnight before they got in. Much of the estate was sold and strict economies were put in place in the castle. More than half of the estate's income went to pay the interest on a huge mortgage. Disputes between the estate and its tenant farmers over rent reductions in the 1880's led to eviction notices, riots in Mitchelstown and the shooting dead of two and the injuring of twenty protesters by the R.I.C. By the turn of the century there were less disputes but the end of the house was in sight. The last garden party was held on the 5th of August 1914, the day after the First World War broke out. During the Civil War the castle was occupied by Anti-Treaty forces who burnt it before retreating from the advancing Free State forces. The estate was sold and the ruin of the castle demolished. The cut stone was used to build the church at Mount Melleray abbey, Co. Waterford in the 1920's. Today miles of the estate boundary walls and some ancillary buildings survive at Mitchelstown .

From a stereoscopic print pair, **Stereoscopic Illustrations**, no. xxxiii,

'Fallow Deer, 1863 3 minutes A.P.A.'

A posed photograph again showing someone from a Big House engaged in field sports. Game hunting and fishing were then and still are controlled. Only the well off had the opportunity to fish or shoot, at least legally. Game was strictly preserved and severe sentences were given to poachers who were caught. Landowners built walls around their properties to protect their game from poachers and their woods from people gathering firewood. Fallow deer were first introduced by the Normans and kept in parks, as the two here may have been, but today most are wild and descended from escapees.

EC Album 1, image 51.

'Salmon Fishing, Rochestown, 1862. 3 seconds'

Rochestown is a few miles south of Cahir, on the River Suir. In 1867 the Wise family lived there and this may be one of the family. The house is now a ruin. The Suir still has some salmon though nothing like it would have had in the past. This photograph would have been taken in the spring or summer of 1862.

EC Album 1, image 33.

1816   4th August, WDH born [183], son of Samuel Hemphill, M.D. of Springhill.

1838   Licentiate, Royal College of Surgery [184].

1839   Samuel Hemphill (father), Physician and Surgeon, 12 Gordon Street, Richard Hemphill at same address[185].

1844   M.D. St. Andrews University, F. and L.M. R.C.S.I.

1849   25th Jan. WDH marries Sarah Henrietta Pedder, Clonmel[186].

1850   15th October, Samuel William Hemphill born to WDH and SP

1851   WDH shows ivory carvings at Great Exhibition, London.

1853   Mary F. Beverley Hemphill born.

1853   Earliest known WDH photograph, Lismore Castle and bridge under repair.

1854   WDH one of three Trustees in leasing land for Horticultural Garden

1856   Lady Osborne, Newtown Anner, dies.

1856   WDH, Upper Johnston Street[187].

1857   WDH photographs St. Mary's Church, Clonmel and (22nd July), dedicates album of St. Mary's views to his brother, the Rev. Richard Hemphill.

1857-8 Summers WDH takes photographs used in **Stereographic Illustrations**.

1858   WDH takes photographs of artefacts on exhibition at Clonmel Art Exhibition.

1858,   30th September, Clonmel Art Exhibition address on photography delivered by WDH.

1858   WDH takes view of crowds at gateway of Horticultural Garden for Clonmel Flower Show [188].

1859   WDH writes foreword for **Stereographic Illustrations**.

1860,   **Stereographic Illustrations** published

1860,   WDH photographs include:

•portrait of a lady (prob. Mrs. Osborne, Newtown Anner, Ex. 642, signed *'W.D.H. Phot. 1860'*)

• *'Odontoglossum Grande'*,

• *'Orchid House W.D.H. 1860 25 minutes. A.PA.'*

1861   WDH photographs include:

•*'Cahir Castle, East. 1861 30 seconds'*

•*'Cahir Castle, West'*,

•*Cahir Castle Entrance Gateway'*,

•*'Cahir Castle North'*,

•*'Cahir Castle and Bridge'*

•*'Ruins of Cathedral' (west end of chancel, Cashel)*,

•*'St. Dominic's Abbey, Cashel'*,

•*' The Slope Newtown Anner'*,

•*'Interior North Transept, Rock of Cashel 1861 3 Minutes'*

•*'Rock of Cashel, NT. East. 1861 15 secs. A.PA. Honble. Mention Gt. Exhibition 1862'*

•*'Flamboyant Window St. Dominics Abbey, Cashel 1861 2 minutes A.PA. Hon: Mention Gt. Exhibition 1862'*

1862   WDH photographs include

- *'Clonmel from Merlin, Sept. 1862 Dry Plate 90 seconds '*
- *'Clonmel'* (view along Clonmel's quay),
- *'The Slope, Newtown Anner 1862, Dry Plate 4 Seconds A.P.A.',*
- *'East Window. St. Mary's, Clonmel 1862 30 seconds',*
- *'Salmon Fishing Rochestown 1862 3 seconds',*
- *'Dendrobium Densiflorum',*
- *'St. Mary's Church, Clonmel. 1862 15 seconds'*
- *'H. B. Pedder, 7th Huzzars'*
- *'H. B. Pedder',*
- *'R. A. officers, Armstrong Gun',*
- *'Colonel Evelegh C.B. 1862',*
- *' Lt. Hamilton, R.A. Capt. Betty. R.A. Lt. Peck RE. Dr. Tait R.A. 1862.10 secs' 1862 Great Exhibition*

Prizes included :

- *'Ruins of Cathedral Rock of Cashel. 1861. 30 secd. Honble. Mention Gt. Exhibition 1862 A.P.A'*
- *'Cahir Castle, Entrance Gateway 15 Sec. 1861 A.P.A. Honorable Mention, Great Exhibition, 1862'*
- *'Cahir Castle & Bridge 60 sec. 1861 APA Hon. Mention Gt. Exhibition 1862'*
- *'Ruins of Cathedral Rock of Cashel. 1861. 30 secd. Honble. Mention Gt. Exhibition 1862 A.P.A'*
- *'Ancient Cross & Entrance Doorway. Rock of Cashel. 1861 65 sec. Hon. Mention. Gt. Exhibn.1862'*
- *'Rock of Cashel, NT. East. 1861 15 secs. A.P.A. Honble. Mention Gt. Exhibition 1862'*
- *'Interior. North Transept, Rock of Cashel. 1861. 3 Minutes. Hon. Mention Gt. Exhib. 1862'*
- *'Flamboyant Window St. Dominics Abbey, Cashel 1861 2 minutes A.P.A. Hon: Mention Gt. Exhibition 1862'*

Family albums record two others, *'Rock of Cashel. South East 1861'* and *'The Slope, Newtown Anner 1861'* as also receiving an Honourable Mention.

1863   WDH photographs include:

- *'View from Dark Walk. Newtownanner, 1863. 25 seconds A.P.A'*
- *'Flower Show, Clonmel'* (April),
- *'From Merlin, Clonmel, July 1863. A.P.A. Dry plate, 30 seconds'*
- *'Ashbourne. Clonmel 1863 A.P.A 30 seconds.'*
- *'Kiltinan Castle, Dry Plate 60 sec. 1863 A.P.A.',*
- *'Holycross Abbey'* and several other Holycross views,
- *'View on River Suir 1863. Dry Plate 60 secs. A.P.A'.*
- *'Flower Show. Clonmel . April 1863 . half secd.',*
- *'Two Mile Bridge. River Anner. 1863.Dry Plate 5 mins. A.P.A',*
- *'Drawing Room W. D. Hemphill. 1863. 25 mins. A.P.A. (Brighton Place), '*
- *'Roman Girl 1863. 25 sect. A.P.A'*
- *'Spanish Lady' 1863 20 seconds A.P.A.'*
- *'Market Girl' Tipperary. 1863 20 seconds A.P.A.'*
- *'Fallow Deer. 1863. 3 mins. A.P.A.',*
- *'District Lunatic Asylum , Clonmel . 12 secs. 1863',*
- *'Clonmel. 1863. Dry Plate 30 seconds'* (A circular print with trees in foreground framing parts of houses and buildings along the quay)

Prize: Amateur Photographic Association Honourable Mention
1864.   WDH photographs include:

- •*'Drawing Room Newtown Anner, 1st Prize Amateur Phot. Association 1864' Prize Medal (specially mentioned) International Exhibition. Dublin 1865',*
- •*'View from Dining – room Newtown Anner. A.P.A 1864. 8 seconds',*
- •*' The Oatfield , 1864. 7 seconds.'*
- •*'Rebekah & Eliezer . 1864. 4 seconds',*
- •*'Judith with Holofernes' head. 1864. 7 secs',*
- •*' The Opera box. 1864 7 sec',*
- •*'Officers and Non-Com. Officers, R.A.',*
- •*'Group on Col. Evelegh's steps. 1864 12 secs',*
- •*'Group taken at Lakefield, 1864'* (Royal Artillery on camp, group with family members),
- •*'Royal Artillery Firing, 1864. 1 second',*
- •*'May' 20 sec. 1864"* (his daughter),
- •*'Miss Grace Osborne 1864 12 seconds',*
- •*'S. W. Hemphill 1864 7 sects'* (his son),
- •*'Autumn & Summer Fruit. 1864. 2 minutes. Wothlytype.',*
- •*'Spezzia Girl. 1864. 20secs.',*
- •*'Firing Royal Salute Queen's Birthday 1864.',*
- •*'From New Bridge, _ second. A.P.A.',*
- •*'Ash Trees, Newtown Anner, 1864'*
- •*'Group of exotics, Clonmel Flower Show, June 1864, 7 minutes'.*

Prizes received:
Amateur Photographic Association 1st Prize Gold Medal 1864 for 'Drawing Room Newtown Anner'
Amateur Photographic Association Honourable Mention 1864
Ruined Abbeys and Castles of Great Britain and Ireland by William Howitt, published in London this year, containing five Hemphill images.
1865   WDH photographs include:

- •*'Marlfield House, 1865',*
- •*'Drawing Room, Marlfield 1865. 25 minutes',*
- •*'Orchid House 1865',*
- •*'Walnut & Ash Trees Newtown Anner. 1865. 7 secs.',*
- •*'At Newtown Anner 1865 6 secs'* (landscape view framed by trees in the demesne with two men posed in front, one sitting by a tree the other with a shotgun and a hare or rabbit).
- •*'Drawing Room, Marlfield, 1865, 25 minutes',*
- •*'The Hall – Marlfield 1865. 30 minutes.'*
- •*'Drawing room - Marlfield . 1865. 25 minutes.'*
- •*'Marlfield .1865 20 seconds.'*
- •*'Marlfield from the Co. Waterford road. 1865. 30 secs.'*
- •*'Ash trees at Newtown Anner .. 1865. 3 minutes',*
- •*'At Newtown Anner. 1865. 6 secs.',*
- •*'Study – Miss Osborne. 1865. 30 seconds.',*
- •*'Lady Blessington's Bath, 1865. 7 secs. Prize Silver Cup 1866.'*

Prizes received:

International Exhibition Dublin Prize Medal 1865 *'Drawing Room Newtown Anner'*

International Exhibition Dublin Do. for Interior Specified 1865 *'Drawing Room Newtown Anner'*

Amateur Photographic Association Silver Cup   1865

A ' view of Kilmanahan Castle ... was prize picture of 1865' in the Amateur Photographic Association (letter, 15/8/01, Pamela Roberts, Collection Librarian, Royal Photographic Society Bath, TSCM file 16/9) and this may be the prize referred to here.

Amateur Photographic Association Honourable Mention   1865

London Photographic Society   Specially Mentioned by Jury 1865

1866 March 17th, Father, Samuel Hemphill, M.D. dies aged eighty four.

WDH photographs include:

- *'Cedrus Libani" at Newtown Anner. 6 seconds. 1866.',*
- *'Portrait, Evening. 2 minute. 1866.',*
- *'Portrait, Reading. 2 min. 1866.',*
- *'The Artist . 15 secs. 1866.',*
- *'Gurteen . 20secs. 1866.',*
- *' Portrait. Evening. 1866 2 minutes'* and a portrait of a girl in fancy dress, perhaps May Hemphill.

Dedicated and presents copy of Stereoscopic Illustrations presented to his wife, also to son S. W. Hemphill and to M.B.F. (May) Hemphill.

Prizes

Amateur Photographic Association Silver Cup (*for 'Lady Blessington's Bath, 7 Sec 1865'* and (two prizes) Honourable Mention.

1867   WDH photographs include:

- *'White Currants (The Prize of Prizes) 1 minute',*
- *'Our first Drawing – Room. 40seconds. 1867.',*
- *'The Harpist, 10 secs. 1867.',*
- *'Castletown . 40 secs. 1867.'.*

Prizes received:

International Exhibition Paris   Certificate of Honor 1867

Amateur Photographic Association Honourable Mention and prize silver cup and coffee pot *'White Currants. 1 minute. Prize A.P.A. 1867 Paris Exhibition.'* was one of the images awarded prizes.

1870   WDH noted, in Slater's Directory for 1870 as the Physician for the County Gaol and House of Correction

Publication of **Memorials of Lady Osborne** by her daughter, illustrated with WDH prints. Volume one has *View from Dark Walk and View from Dining Room, Newtown Anner,* Volume two has *The Slope, Newtown Anner* (view with several women) and *'Lady Osborne's Summer House'.*

1871   Evelyn Alice Hemphill (dau.) born . WDH buys Oak Ville

1874   Edith Osborne marries Henry Arthur Blake.

1875   WDH presents commercial photograph album to May for Christmas. Publishes article re bloodstains in Dublin Journal of Medical Science. Becomes a Freeman of Clonmel.

1880   Mrs. Osborne dies.

1880-1 Basset's Guide notes WDH physician to County Gaol and Visiting Physician to

Lunatic Asylum and Auxiliary.

1881   May, WDH takes part in a concert in Clonmel Courthouse

1882   Possible photograph by WDH of Oak Ville in family album no. 3. Ralph Bernal
        Osborne dies

1889 or 1890 WDH takes part in a concert in the Parochial Hall, Clonmel.

1889   WDH, Physician, Oakville and Visiting Physician to Lunatic Asylum (Basset)

1891   Several dated views in family album, some if not all by WDH, include'
   - *View from Bedroom Window Oakville'*,
   - *'View of house,*
   - *'From Garden, Oakville'*
   - *'Garden, Oakville'*,
   - *'View of House, Oakville from Terrace Walk'*
   - *'Porch, Oakville, 1891',*
   - *'View from Avenue, 1891'*.

1892   WDH photographs include
   - *'Corner Evelyn's Bedroom',*
   - *'The Library, Oakville',*
   - *'Dining Room, Oakville, 1892',*
   - *'Corner of May's bedroom, 1892',*
   - *'Afternoon tea Corner Drawing Room Oakville, 1892',*
   - *'Dining Room, Oakville, 1892'.*
   - *'From 41 St. Stephens Green Dublin June 1892'*

as well as several other views of Oakville and a similar number of possible WDH images such
as : *'Royal Botanic garden Glasnevin 1892',*

1892   Evelyn Alice Hemphill dies, buried Old St. Mary's, Clonmel, 2 July .

1893   Probable WDH images
   - *'Geometric Garden, Oakville',*
   - *'Orchid House Oakville 1893'.*

1893   M. B. Hemphill dated album of images include ships and locations.

1893   Dr. M.J. Hewetson now Physician to Her Majesty's Prison

1897   Publication of The Yew Trees of Great Britain and Ireland containing
        Hemphill images.

1897   11th November, Sarah Hemphill, WDH's wife dies

1901   May 14th, Samuel William Hemphill, son dies.

1902   Sunday, 13th of July, WDH dies. Buried Old St. Mary's Clonmel, 17th July.

1925   May Hemphill dies, buried Old St. Mary's, Clonmel.

Footnotes

[1] Henceforth WDH. Dr Hemphill sometimes used the monograph WDH but signed himself
as William D. Hemphill. D is for Despard, his grandmother's name. The Hemphill family is
thought to have taken its name from Hemphill near Kilmarnock, Ayrshire in Scotland. At some
stage in the late 16th or early 17th century, Boyd of Hemphill, the founder of the family in
Ireland, moved to Camus near Coleraine. His great grandson, Samuel Hemphill came to
Tipperary in 1728 when he was appointed Presbyterian Minister in Fethard following two years

as Minister in Ballybrittas. He purchased land near Coolnacapogue, Killenaule where he built a house called Springhill. The house remained in the family until 1945 when it was sold after the death of Henry Hemphill.

William Despard Hemphill was fourth in the family of six boys and three girls of Samuel Hemphill M.D. and Mary Backas. His eldest brother Edward inherited Springhill Estate and never married. When he died he was succeeded by his brother Robert. One of Robert's sons later became one of the first members of the new Tipperary S.R. County Council in 1899, having been nominated by the superseded Grand Jury . The next brother, Richard, was an author and theologian who for forty five years was Minister of the North Strand Church, Dublin. A selection of his writings entitled **Fragments** was edited by his son Richard and published in 1888. Samuel the fifth brother became a solicitor in Dublin, married Charlotte Cathcart and established the firm of Cathcart and Hemphill. John became a clergyman. Ellen married Daniel Foley and Frances married Basil Aldwell whose son Basil later became Rector of Portsmouth. Their sister Mary died quite young in 1849. I am grateful to the Hemphill family for this information.

[2] Irish Medical Directory, Dublin, 1874-6, 87, RIA.

[3] Obit. 1

[4] A fourth child, Colyn Alice, born 14th December, 1870 and baptised 28th January 1871 may have died soon after. St. Mary's (Church of Ireland) Parish Records, Clonmel. Letter dated 23rd July 2002.

[5] Cusack 1984.

[6] Obit. 1.

[7] Family Scrapbook.

[8] Hemphill 1860, xv-xxxiii.

[9] Obit.1.

[10] Hemphill 1860, xxxii.

[11] Cusack 1984.

[12] O'Donnell 1999, 266.

[13] See 1839, **The New Commercial Directory for the cities of Waterford and Kilkenny and the towns of Clonmel, Carrick-on-Suir, New Ross and Carlow**, F. Kinder & Son, 1856, **Slater's Directory of Ireland**, 1870, **Slater's Dir**. 1870 and 1880-81**County Tipperary Directory**. W. Basset, 1886, **Francis Guy's Directory of Munster**, and other directories all in Tipperary County Library, Thurles.

[14] Ex. 665, collection of documents acquired by South Tipperary County Museum.

[15] Cusack 1984.

[16] O'Donnell 1999, 10-11.

[17] Ex. 665.

[18] Obit. 1.

[19] A set of photographs which was purchased for the library of the Royal Society of Antiquaries (**Proceedings, J. Roy. Soc, Antiq. Ire. Vol 1 New Series, Part 2. 1857, 360**) cannot now be located (letter, N.M.F. Arnould, Librarian, R.S.A.I to author, 19th Jan. 2001) but they were probably identical to those in the album he presented to his brother in 1857.

[20] **Proceedings, J. Roy.Soc.Antiq, Ser. 2, Vol 111, part 1, 1860-1, 170**

[21] Ibid, p 192,

[22] Family clippings album, copy in TSCM files, 16/9/33.1.

[23] Obit.1.

[24] Ex. 552, **Catalogue of Clonmel Art Exhibition**, 1858.

[25] Obit.1

[26] Ex. 645, South Tipperary Co. Museum.

[27] EC album 1, 17b, National Photographic Archive, Chandler Coll. Nos, 1 and 2, no. 3 show the Garden in winter (no. 3) and the show at the Garden from a top window of his nearby house in 1863 (nos. 1 and EC album 1, 17b , identical) and from the street (no. 2) in 1858 .

[28] Nelson and McCracken 1987,40, 56.

[29] He gave gifts of seeds and plants to Glasnevin on a few occasions (information courtesy Dr. Peadar Slattery)

[30] Will dated 20th January, 1909. Ex 665

[31] Susan Bennett, Curator of the Royal Society of Arts, London, has informed me that there is an entry for Hemphill in 'volume 2 of the Official Descriptive and Illustrated Catalogue of the Great Exhibition, 1851, Class 28, Manufactures from animal, no.158' as follows: 'Hemphill, W.D., Clonnel (sic), Ireland, Designer and Manufacturer: a vase in the Elizabeth style; a miniature frame; a vase, after the antique, with lily of the valley and fuschia; and twelve dessert knife-handles, of various designs; all executed in ivory. A candlestick and match-holder, in African blackwood and ivory. A small vase, after the antique, in walrus ivory, showing the beautiful reticulated appearance of the interior of the tooth when turned extremely thin; a small cup, in the same material, showing the great strength of the enamel of the tooth of which the slender pillar is turned; vases in hippopotamus ivory' (email to author, Nov. 23rd, 2000).

[32] 260 EC Album 5 14 group of ivory turning, Great Exhibition, 1851.

[33] Ex. 552, Catalogue of Clonmel Art Exhibition , 1858.

[34] Obit. 1.

[35] Girouard 1992, 129. An image of several pieces of old Waterford Glass is among his photographs (EC Album 5, 13).

[36] Copy in family scrapbook

[37] O'Donnell 1999, 266

[38] Obit. 2

[39] Cusack 1984

[40] Obit.1

[41] ibid

[42] Hayes 1989, 6.

[43] Eva, an independently minded woman, had spent most of her youth at boarding school following the death of her father. She went to London to do war work for much of the 1914-18 war. She was engaged to marry one of the sons of Edward Hackett, then County Surveyor. However a cutting pasted into a family album records: 'Hackett, in loving memory of Eric A. N. Hackett, 2nd Lieutenant R. I. Regiment killed in Ginchy battle, 9th of September, 1916 and of L. Aylmer H. Hackett M. C. Captain, Royal Irish Rifles and Royal Munster Fusiliers killed at Ypres on 24th April 1918 and of Venice C. Hackett died on 13th October, 1918 brave lives given in the Great War and of Teddy F. Hackett died on 9th July 1915 and his twin sister, Alma Evelyn, loving wife of Gerald N. F. Barry, died on 25th of September, 1918 devoted children of Edward and Emily Hackett, Ballanagh, Avoca and late of Castletown Park, Ballycumber.'

Edward Hackett retired as County Surveyor for Tipperary S.R. in April, 1920 having also served the Grand Jury for some ten years prior to their dissolution in 1899. He was the youngest son of Thomas Hackett of Castlearmstrong, Co. Offaly and had trained as a mechanical engineer. 'It is clear that while the Council had inherited him from the old Ascendency Regime, with which he himself identified, he was an excellent and dedicated official of the Council. On the occasion of his retirement, Councillors, while allowing that they might disagree with him politically, paid tribute to his courtesy and sterling worth' (Long 1999, 49). Edward Hackett saw all his children predecease him. Venice died in the great influenza epidemic. The Land Commission broke up the estate and Edward Hackett, by now a widower, sold the house to the County Council who demolished it to crush its stones for road chippings.. He died in February, 1945 being preceded by the last of his family, Geraldine his daughter, in February 1943 (Devine 1989, 138, 141, TSCM file 25/56).

[44]Ex.665

[45]Cusack 1984

[46]The photographs show members of foot batteries of the Royal Artillery, apparently the 8th Battery, 8th Brigade (The battery designation can be seen painted on the trail of the gun in one photograph dated to 1862 (EC Album 1.42/40)) though this battery was renamed as H Battery on the 9th of June, 1861. Perhaps the authorities decided not to repaint the unit name on the guns though this seems somewhat unmilitary. I would like to thank Matthew Buck of the Royal Artillery Museum for his assistance (email to author, September 10th, 2001).

[47]Girouard 1992, 125.

[48]ibid. 121 et seq.

[49]Bence-Jones 1996, 210.

[50]Girouard 1992, 130, also see her letters in Osborne 1870.

[51]Ralph Bernal added his wife's name to his own on marriage.

[52]O' Donnell 1999, 12.

[53]Girouard 1992, 133 quoting the Dictionary of National Biography.

[54]O'Donnell 1999, 281.

[55]Osborne 1870, Volume One, pps 52, 97, 98. He was also consulted during the fatal illness of Sir Thomas' son, William in May 1824 (ibid, 61). Sir Thomas is reputed to have first consulted a vet.

[56]Osborne 1870, Vol. One, 307.

[57]Letter from Mr Eric Earle, Guildford, noting that at Hatfield House (to where the contents of Newtown Anner were brought) is a press cutting 'Splendid Fete at Newtown in celebration of Miss Osborne's attaining her majority, July 3rd, 1839. Among 'numerous gentry who were present were ..... John Bagwell, John Power, Gurteen, Col. Greene and family, Kilmanahan Castle, Henry Pedder, Oakville' (file 16/9, TSCM).

[58]Osborne 1870, Volume One, p. 97.

[59]Ex. 552, Catalogue of Clonmel Art Exhibition , 1858.

[60]Hemphill 1860.

[61]Dodier 1999, 24

[62]Volume One has *View from the Dining Room* as the frontispiece and *View from Dark Walk* on the title page. Volume Two has *The Slope Newtown Anner* and *View of the Temple, Lady Osborne's Summer House.*

[63]Crookshank and Glin 1994, 119

[64]Girouard 1992, 130.

[65]Butler 1990,137, Crookshank and Glin 1994, 119.

[66]Lot 166 in Whytes Auction of 13th Jan 2001, contained some family papers with the information that he was born in Limerick in 1840 and was Governor of the Bahamas, Newfoundland, Queensland, Hong Kong and Ceylon. His marriage to Edith was his second. The New York Times of 11th November, 1888 described him as *'one of the numerous landlord family of that name in Connaught, was seven years ago a poor sub-inspector in the Irish Constabulary, but a handsome young fellow, who ran away with and married the elder daughter of Bernal Osborne. Her younger sister had just before wedded the Duke of St. Albans, and by the influence of this ducal connection Blake was made one of the five district magistrates on whom the working of the coercion act of 1882 devolved. .... He made himself so fiercely hated by the people that he had to be removed from Ireland. ... Blake leaped full-fledged into the dignity of Governor of the Bahamas. When the Duke of St. Albans ratted from Gladstone as a Liberal Unionist a part of the price he secured from the Tories was Blake's advancement to the Governorship of Newfoundland, and now the effort is made further to promote him to Queensland. Even the Ministerial Standard to-day attacks the Colonial Office for its stupidity in thus, against numerous warnings, provoking a quarrel with the colony, and this may suffice to secure the withdrawal of an appointment that is resented by every Irishman in Australia'* (http://www.casebook.org/press_reports/new_york_times/nytnov11.html 27/6/01). In the early years of her marriage Edith published a book on **The Realities of Freemasonry** (Butler 2000) a most unusual achievement as women were not admitted to the Masons. I would like to thank Dr. Karlene Kenefik for this reference.

[67]Elwood and Harvey 1990, 148,151.

[68]Butler 1990, 88

[69]Butler 2000, also see Ellwood and Harvey, 1990.

[70]Ibid 137. It is unlikely that the watercolour of Catherine Osborne's coming of age attributed to Grace by Butler (1990, 137) is in fact by her, as Crookshank and Glin (1994,143) have pointed out. She probably inscribed the label as an identification rather than an attribution.

[71]Excerpt from memoir by member of the Bagwell family, partial copy in South Tipperary County Museum Ex.595.

[72]Girouard 1992,134

[73]Obit. 2

[74]Heyert 1979, 111.

[75]Seiberling 1986, 4.

[76]Chandler and Walsh, 6

[77]Seiberling 1986, 2

[78]Davison 1989

[79]David Davison, letter, to E. Earle, 13th January, 1986, copy in file 25/15 TSCM.

[80]Sexton 1994

[81]A number of ladies from Clonmel and Lismore founded a watercolour society in 1870 and one of them, Miss Currey of Lismore Castle, was a friend of the Osborne sisters (Crookshank and Glin, 1994, 221, Butler 2000, 114). Miss Currey was probably a daughter of F.E. Currey, the photographer. Art Exhibitions were held in Lismore and Clonmel in 1871 and it is clear that there was an active amateur art movement locally. Mrs. Osborne sent several works of art for display and Grace Osborne exhibited her own work. Both Mrs. Osborne and Mr. Currey were

honorary members of the Amateur Art Society. While WDH is not mentioned specifically he must have moved in the same circles and have visited the exhibitions. Both Currey and WDH were members of the APA (Chandler 2001, 34) and I strongly believe, though I have no definite proof, that they knew each other.

[82]Holland 1999.

[83]Dodier, 1999

[84]Lawson 1997,4, Dodier, 1999, 21

[85]A second photographer can be seen in a stereo photograph taken by Lady Hawarden at Dundrum (Dodier 1999, 220) in 1857 or 1858. She left Dundrum in 1859 and went on to use full plate negatives from then on.

[86]Copy letter, file 16/9 TSCM, Dodier to E. Earle, 8th August, 1999.

[87]Dodier 1999, 24

[88]This suggestion is supported by the fact that Lady Osborne, while living in a Big House, albeit a socially isolated one, some twenty miles away from Dundrum, had not met Lord Hawarden (Osborne 1879, Vol, One, 207).

[89]Chandler 2001, 8.

[90]Obit 1.

[91]A note which used to exist in family possession (Information from Eric Earle re: a record of family matters kept by Henry Hemphill of Springhill, not now located) recorded that his case at the Great Exhibition of 1851 in London had included photographs. There is certainly a photograph entitled 'Group of ivory turning, Great Exhibition, 1851' (EC Album 5 14) among his prints but there is no evidence that he took the photograph and there are no photographs shown.

[92]EC Album 2.8a

[93]A photograph taken the day after the collapse has been published by Sexton (1994, 21)

[94]Mealys' (1995) dating of a photograph as a 'Contemporary photographic portrait of Thomas Graham, c. 1850 by Hemphill Photographer, Clonmel' seems a bit early. A modern copy has generously been given by Mealys to South Tipperary County Museum (1996.93).

[95]Hemphill 1860, ix.

[96]'Anner Castle'. An oval view from a good viewpoint with a few trees. A stereograpic card with this image, the second looser foliage frame, monogramme, gold print is illustrated by Chandler (2001, 38).

[97]Copies were generously provided by Mr. E Earle and are now in the Co. Museum.

[98]Generously loaned by the present owner of Newtown Anner to the Co. Museum (Ex. 640).

[99]A letter of Lady Osborne's (Osborne 1870, Vol. One 263) mentions Jaccard (sic) making out a list of servants' wages.

[100]There are at least two portraits of a lady who is probably Mrs. Osborne in the conservatory at Newtown Anner. One (South Tipperary County Museum Ex. 343) has her with a light-coloured bonnet and holding a parasol, while leaning on a small balustrade, image mounted on card with WDH monogram. Another (Ex.642.11) is a stereoscopic print pair, on better quality cream card of a woman seated at a table, with plants about, a small balustrade in the foreground and a window in the background. The book on the table is **Stereoscopic Illustrations** open at the frontispiece print of the Round Tower at the Rock of Cashel. The reverse has, in ink (non-modern) the inscription 'W.D.H. Phot. 1860' and in faded ink or pencil below 'A. P. H.' The

first inscription is probably by WDH himself. A very similar if not identical (to Ex. 642.11) image has been published by Sexton (2002, 59) as being Mrs Osborne taken by John Lawrence, c. 1860. While the subject is correct, I wonder about the photographer, given the signature.

[101]'*Rev. Richard Hemphill from his affect. brother WDH Clonmel July 22nd, 1857'*. This item is in the collections of the County Museum (1995.905). A similar, but not unique, example of an antiquarian recording a historic church, St. Fin Barre's Cathedral in Cork, photographed by Thomas R. Lane in 1865, has been published by Rynne and Wigham (2002).

[102]Quinlan 2001

[103]Seiberling 1986, 4.

[104]It measures 11.2 cm by 18.3 cm (Part of Ex. 343). To the list of dedicatees given in the leaflet can be added the remainder as listed in Stereoscopic Illustrations: iv. Lismore, His Grace the (late) Duke of Devonshire, v. Lismore Sir Joseph Paxton, M.P., vi. Holycross The Rev. C.W. Wall D.D.,Vice Provost, T.C.D. vii. Holycross, The (late) Hon. Baron Pennefather, viii Clonmel, John Bagwell, Esq., M.P. , ix Kiltinane &c., Mrs. Osborne, Newtown Anner, x Newtown Anner, R. B. Osborne, Esq., M.P. , xi Shanbally Castle, &c. Right Hon. the Vicountess Lismore., xii Athassil Abbey, the Rev. James Graves, Hon. Sec. Kilkenny Archaeological Society., xiii Cahir, Right Hon. the Countess of Glengall., xiv, Clonmel, The Rev. J. Bury Palliser, Formerly Rector of Clonmel., xv Marlfield, the Hon. Mrs Bagwell., xvi Curraghmore, The Most Noble Louisa, Marchioness of Waterford, xvii Knocklofty, The Right Hon. the Countess of Donoughmore xviii Slate Quarries, &c., William Stokes, Esq., M.D. M.R.I.A., Dublin. xix Antiquities G. Petrie, Esq., LL. D. , M.R.I.A. xx Mitchelstown Castle His Excellency the Earl of Carlisle, Lord Lieutenant of Ireland.

[105]Part of Ex.343.

[106]Loose pre-printed pages, some with stereographs tipped in, are also known (Part of Ex.343). They may have been available separately.

[107]Irish Architectural Archive no. 2000.119. I am very grateful for permission to see this item

[108]On page 100 of the Brunskill album (Scarry 1997) is a stereograph, on green card with a pre-printed floral frame and monogram showing 'Athassil Abbey, East', identical to no xxiv in **Stereoscopic Illustrations.**

[109]Both frames are of branches with foliage and fruit but one is different in being much more ornate with intertwined limbs and leaves on either side and heavy swirling curvilinear motifs on top and bottom, a large or small monogram in a space above a lion's mask centrally placed above the prints. Chandler (2001, 38) shows a stereographic card with the looser foliage frame and monogram. One card has the gold foliage frame printed over part of the image (Ex. 642, no. 8).

[110]Commercial stereographs, often printed on yellow card, also exist of scenes such as the Rock of Cashel as Hemphill himself noted in the foreword to **Stereoscopic Illustrations.** However the absence of the monogram and foliage frame does not necessarily mean that the images are not by WDH.

[111]A stereograph (Ex. 642, no. 7) is inscribed 'Front of Uncle Wms. House in Johnston Street'. The Brunskill album (Scarry 1997) contains a large number of antiquarian photographs including four Hemphill images. It shows that Hemphill work was available to a collector in the Kilkenny area in the late 19th century.

[112]There is a slightly differing title on a page, with stereograph, before the actual title page.

[113]1983.350

[114]He may be the artist who illuminated the dedication. One of his daughters was also artistic. A newspaper clipping in an album which may have belonged to his wife (EC Family clippings album, copy in TSCM files, 16/9/33.1) notes that Miss Hemphill of Oak Ville had executed an illuminated address, dated Easter 1881 for presentation to the retiring organist of St. Mary's, Mr. Thomas Stanistreet.

[115]The book also has a secondary dedication, 'James White, Gortnafleur, Clonmel' hand-written in black, on the reverse of the page with first dedication:

[116]He is careful to point out in a footnote that the first numbers of 'this work' (meaning probably the 20 separate parts) were issued before Piazzi Smith's publication on Tenerife and also to point out that he had photographed Cashel and Holycross, before the Stereoscopic Company of London and others.

[117]**Stereoscopic Illustrations**, 95

[118]Given the differences found between the two copies in the County Museum it may be of interest to those lucky enough to have access to a copy of **Stereoscopic Illustrations** to have a list of the illustrations in his wife's copy for comparison.

1. **Panoramic View of Cashel from the Rock.**
The Palace of the Church of Ireland Archbishops of Cashel and the gardens surrounding it are prominent in this view of Cashel from a distance.

2. **General View - North-east.**
A fine picturesque view of the Rock and the buildings on it. A gentleman with top hat sits in a field in the foreground and, in the middle ground, some houses run along a roadway.

3. **General View – South-east.**
A closer view of the Rock and its buildings behind the graveyard wall, with several thatched cottages behind a roadside wall. There are no people visible. The high roadside wall and the blocked gateway in it all give an impression of exclusion.

4. **General View from the Palace Gardens.**
Probably taken from an upper floor window of the Archbishop's Palace, this view shows the gardens, with a family posed in the left foreground and the Rock appearing above the high trees.

5. **Ancient Cross and Entrance Doorway.**
Two carefully posed gentlemen, one well dressed, leaning his head upon his stick in front of St. Patrick's Cross, the other drawing one's eye to the centrally located Cathedral doorway where he is standing. The difference in their sizes points out the distance between them and the scale of the features they are positioned beside. Deep areas of shadow, a feature of WDH's work, add depth to the buildings in the background.

6. **View of Cormac's Chapel – Exterior.**
A reclining gentleman, gives scale to the leaning headstones around him while, in the background, lichen and vegetation mottle the exterior of Cormac's Chapel.

7. **South-west View.**
Several people are posed at the base of the walls of the buildings in the south-western part of the Rock. One gentleman is standing on top of a large lump of masonry.

8. **Round Tower and North View.**
This view is in the same location as the photograph of Dr. Hemphill and one of his cameras in front of the Round Tower used as the frontispiece. Here the human interest is provided by a

gentleman dramatically pointing with his stick towards the Cathedral.

9. North Transept and Great Arches – Interior.
This location was photographed at least twice by Dr. Hemphill. A better photograph, reproduced in this book, taken in 1861, is a carefully posed view, a study of light and dark, lines and texture in the interior of the cathedral with two gentlemen placed in the prominent pools of light. This image is similar but inferior with less light and less well placed spectators.

10. Cormac's Chapel - Interior.
A ray of light from the later window lights the gloomy interior of the Chancel of Cormac's Chapel.

11. View of Remains of Eastern Window and Choir.
Taken from high up under the crossing, this view shows the long choir of the Cathedral with the gaping space at the end where the east window once stood.

12. View of Hoare Abbey through the Circular Window.
Taken from a round window in the great tower at the western end of the Cathedral, this mottled view shows us not only Hore abbey but also a rare view of the Tipperary countryside of 1857-8. Regular fields and an absence of woodlands or prominent trees are to be noted.

2. Holycross

13. General View – East from the River.
Two ladies in front of ruined Holy Cross Abbey with the River Suir flowing through reed beds in the foreground

14. Southern View – Exterior.
Ivy choked walls and door-less arches are the main features of this view of the ruins. The two ladies are above, on first floor level, on a grassy level part.

15 View of Arch in Cemetery field.
A lady, with hat and bag, sits in the shadows in the decorated doorway to what was probably the chapter house at Holycross.

16 Western View – Exterior.
Two ladies posing in a hayfield directly outside the western gable of the nave.

17 Western View- Interior.
In contrast to the previous view the interior of the nave is overgrown and deep in shadow from a strong sun.

18 Southern View – Interior.
A view, taken more or less successfully against strong sunlight, of the night stairs leading from the centre of the church to the domestic buildings.

19 Eastern View – Interior.
A view of the interior of one of the side chapels in the southern transept of the church showing the possible shrine and then modern headstones later removed in the 20th century restoration to the nearly cemetery.

20 View of the Sedilia.
This elaborate sedilia or seating place for clergymen is one of the notable features of Holycross with its English royal and Butler family coats of arms. As in the preceding image, the interior of the church is filled with modern headstones and tombs of those families anxious to be buried in long-consecrated ground.

3. Athassil

21 General View of Athassil Abbey.

Two patient ladies posed in front of the gateway to Athassel Augustinian Priory, one of the largest medieval monasteries in Ireland.

22 Arch leading to the Choir.

Two ladies again, seated among the rubble and foliage either side of the west doorway of the chancel at Athassel.

23 Athassil Abbey – West.

A view, looking through a partially blocked gateway towards the western end of the church at Athassel.

24 Athassil – East.

The two ladies yet again, standing in the field to the east of Athassel with behind them the wall enclosing both the church and its ancillary buildings as well as a large tree.

4. Lismore

25 Lismore Castle – North.

A view of the castle, high above the river Blackwater with one tower in the course of construction.

26 Lismore Castle – South.

A view from the gardens towards the castle.

27 Lismore Castle – East.

Again a closer view of the buildings with a fountain to the right.

28 Lismore Castle and Bridge.

A fine and well posed view of a man (? fishing) standing in the rocky shallows of the river with a bridge and the castle in the background. The masonry of the second span of the bridge seems brighter. This is probably a sign of the rebuilding of several spans after their collapse in a flood on November 2nd, 1853. The damaged bridge was photographed by Currey (Sexton 1994, 21) and Hemphill.

29 Lismore Castle, through the Entrance Gateway.

As with most of WDH's Lismore images, this view has no people and shows an empty avenue leading to the castle.

30 View from Drawing-room Window.

A fine view of the main span of the bridge, which survived the 1853 flood (Guinness and Ryan 1971, 283).

31 View of Cathedral Spire from Carlisle Tower.

A view across the chimneys of Lismore Castle towards the spire of St. Carthage's Church of Ireland cathedral.

32 View of Lismore from the Mitchelstown Road

Several persons, ladies, gentlemen and a child arranged somewhat awkwardly on a slope with the upper parts of Lismore castle showing above trees in the background.

5. Mitchelstown

33 Mitchelstown Castle - East.

The stark and new-looking castle, seen from a hayfield in front of the main entrance.

34 Mitchelstown Castle - South.

A view of another side of the building but this time softened by a tree and uncut hay in the field.

35 Mitchelstown Castle - North.

A distant view with the upper parts of the castle seen above trees.

6. Ardfinnan

36 View of Ardfinnan Castle from the River.
The castle, main tower on the right, fragmentary walls on the left, seen from across the Suir with industrial buildings at the river's edge.

37 Interior of the "Lady Abbey", Ardfinnan.
A deeply shadowed study of the interior of this small and somewhat overgrown Carmelite Friary with a lady seated at the base of the crossing arch.

7. Cahir

38 Cahir Castle and Bridge.
Dr. Hemphill took this view a number of times but here captured the castle's reflections in the still waters behind the weir. A number of people are standing on the bridge, looking at the photographer.

39 Cahir Castle – East.
The ivy-covered castle is seen at the bottom of a wide and traffic-less Castle Street with a few passers by and one man centrally placed, directly in front of the most prominent part of the castle.

40 View from Cahir Castle.
Several of Dr. Hemphill's interests coincide in this view of the railway viaduct, St. Paul's Church of Ireland parish church, the river with a row of trees along the banks and the castle with visitors on the wall-walk.

41 Interior of the Choir, Augustinian Abbey, Cahir.
The overgrown interior and eastern window of the Augustinian priory.

42 Cahir Cottage.
Three people, a woman seated on a chair and two children in front of the well kept and ivy-covered Swiss Cottage cottage orné.

43 View in Kilcommon.
A beautiful scene of the River Suir flowing between wooded banks with in the distance the bridge leading to the Swiss Cottage.

8. Clonmel

View of Clonmel from the Mountain. (Title – Page Vignette).
A very small but interesting view of the town with the countryside beyond.

44 View of Clonmel from Merlin.
A well-chosen viewpoint showing the impressive garden, a glimpse of the river and the new bridge between the trees and in the distance, the houses and roofs of Clonmel.

45 New Bridge and Mountain.
Almost the reverse of the last image, this one shows the quays, the new bridge and beyond it, Merlin house and the trees in the gardens of the prosperous Coleville Road. While some of the men on the quay are posed or at least immobile, looking at the photographer who is in an upper window of a house, other, especially the children are blurred. A rowboat is in mid-stream.

46 Quay, through the Arch of the Bridge.
One of the best known of Dr. Hemphill's images, this photograph must be the result of much thought and effort. A view of the quays in Clonmel is framed by an arch of the new bridge. A man on the quays fends off a barge containing a cargo of coal. A man is posed in the bow.

Above, on the bridge, a gas light is being worked on by two men. All seems very busy, plausible and casual. But some, at least, must be posed and planned by the photographer.

47 St. Mary's Church - West.

The western end and porch of Dr. Hemphill's parish church which he photographed several times during his life. Deep shadows among the headstones and trees on either side frame the lighter building in front of which is a man in profile to give scale.

48 St. Mary's Church - Eastern Window

The eastern window, 15th century in date (Quinlan 2001) with a man again in profile to give scale and darker shadowy headstones in the foreground. A similar photograph, but with a different man as scale is in the Brunskill Album (Scarry 1997).

49 Scots' Church – Anglesey – street.

Three or four men standing outside the Church in a quiet street. A horse-drawn vehicle left in the street is probably a Bianconi long car.

50 Model School.

This photograph was probably taken from an upper window of the end house on the southern side of Anne Street, Clonmel. Four ladies are standing on the grass inside the wall which encloses the houses at their western end. Behind the wall we can see an area of nursery gardens and, further away, the Model National School, built in 1849 (Ahearn 1996, 110) and the newer Union Workhouse, completed in 1853 (Lonergan 2000, viii).

51 Railway Station.

Like the buildings in the last photograph, the Railway Station was relatively new when WDH photographed it in 1857/8. It does not appear to be posed as the passengers on the platform are moving and so is a rare documentary Hemphill photograph.

52 View of Clonmel from the Heywood Road.

A general view of Clonmel taken from the higher ground on the Heywood Road. Two girls and a man are posed in the field in the foreground. Behind them is the rear of the Fever Hospital, erected in 1818 (Lonergan 2000, 26). Further to the left are the houses of Queen Street. The tower of St. Mary's Church of Ireland and Saints Peter and Paul Catholic Church stand out against the skyline of the Comeragh foothills, lined with field walls and bare of trees or bushes.

9. Minor Antiquities

53 Western Doorway – Donaghmore Church.

The remains of the Romanesque doorway to Donaghmore Church, a few miles to the north of Clonmel are shown here, with no trace of the previously recorded tymphanum or panel above the door decorated with a two-tailed cat.

54 St. Patrick's Well.

St. Patrick's Well has been altered somewhat in at least two renovations since this photograph was taken but its essential feature, a strong spring flowing through outlets in a low-lying area is still the same. The old lady sitting behind the tree probably hoped for some money from visitors.

55 Old Church – St. Patrick's Well.

A view through the doorway of the church (Romanesque decoration visible on one of the jambs) with various carved stones from a demolished White family memorial chapel at St. Mary's Church of Ireland in Clonmel stacked up against the far gable as they still are today.

56 Cromleac at Gurteen

A portal tomb, or Stone Age burial chamber in the woods of an estate near Kilsheelan consisting of a very large capstone balanced on other large rocks. This photograph has no people in it but a probable Hemphill image in the Brunskill album has a woman and a young boy in front.

10. Scenery and Country Seats.

57 Lady Osborne's Summer-house.
A classical temple surrounded by woods and reflected in the surface of an artificial water channel.

58 The Temple, Newtown Anner.
The same temple, seen from the side, with a woman standing at the bottom of steps leading up from a moored boat to the summer house.

59 View from Dark Walk, Newtown Anner.
A woman sits, leaning against a large ornamental flower pot. The Temple summer house is visible at the end of a long walkway lined with large potted plants. A second woman stands in the walkway to provide a scale.

60 The Slope, Newtown Anner.
Members of the Osborne family along a walkway beside, and in a boat on, the water course in the garden. This view is one that WDH returned to several times until he had achieved the perfect arrangement of people, water, light and reflections. The persons here could be Lady Osborne, her daughter Catherine Osborne and her grand-children Grace and Edith. However Lady Osborne died in 1856, perhaps shortly before these stereographs were taken and another adult may be present with the girls and their mother.

61 The Geometric Garden, Newtown.
The Osborne girls and an adult, their mother perhaps, beside a gravel path in the gardens at Newtown Anner. Two servant girls are sweeping the path and beyond it is a geometric garden with symmetric paths and beds. Beyond it again is the open landscape of the demesne with a water feature of some sort on the left and what may be a glasshouse in the distance.

62 The Steps, Newtown Anner.
Arranged with a considered eye, there are ten women on the wide steps in the garden. Two sets of three in the front, both arranged in a triangle and the others in the background arranged on a further set of steps linking the terraces. This set of steps was used again by WDH.

63 Sir Thomas Osborne's Bridge, River Suir.
A view of the River Suir with Sir Thomas' bridge, linking the family estate at Newtown Anner with their old residence at Tikincor in the far distance. The river and photograph are bounded by vegetation and trees and a lady sits on the bank, apparently oblivious of the photographer.

64 View at Glenpatrick Slate Quarries.
A far off road, with some pedestrians posed on it, winds its way through coniferous woods with a disused and flooded quarry in the foreground. Bushes and trees again frame the photograph.

65 Marlfield House, North.
A gentleman sits on a garden seat outside the large glass house looking out over the lawn and wooded demesne.

66 View at Marlfield.
A man, in trousers and shirt, stands, back to the camera, on the wooded lawn in front of the house.

67 Marlfield, from the River.

A view of the wide River Suir with Marlfield House visible on the other side in the far distance, framed by trees. On this bank, below and close to the photographer, is a coach and coachman.

68 Croquet Ground, Marlfield.

A croquet party of at least eighteen people, all carefully arranged, standing, sitting, reclining on the lawn beside the house. An archery target in the background provided another sport suitable for mixed company.

69 Entrance Gateway, Knocklofty.

A gatekeeper stands to attention inside the partly open gate. A woman stands in front of the gate lodge. The gate piers are decorated with ornate finials and armorial plaques.

70 The Avenue, Knocklofty.

A long avenue framed by magnificent trees on which a single man with top hat is walking away with a woman seated on the verge nearer to the camera.

71 The Bridge, Knocklofty.

A typical and beautiful WDH image, a still river reflecting the bridge and the man perched on its parapet. A large tree on the left hand frames the image. The bridge's masonry looks newly pointed

72 Salmon Leap, Curraghmore,

A figure beside a fence looks down a wooded river valley to where a small waterfall is the central feature in the image.

73 View at Curraghmore,

A distant view of the house, framed by trees, both distant and near, with a lawn and seated figure in the mid-ground to give scale. An iron fence immediately in front of the camera provides interesting patterns and gives a sense of enclosure and of exclusion.

74 Ancient Bridge, Curraghmore,

Again an old bridge is reflected in the still waters of a river. The whole image is framed by foliage and trees. Two men are beside the base of one of the bridge's piers acting as a point of interest in the landscape and also as a scale.

75 Curraghmore House.

A view of the garden front of the house, looking out over the somewhat severe garden of lawns set with an occasional small tree and separated by wide gravel paths. The foreground is filled with a row of small ornamental bushes.

11. Castellated Residences.

76 Kiltinane Castle.

The castle, sited on a rock overlooking the Clashawley River, all framed by trees and foliage.

77 Shanbally Castle.

The large building is set against a background of trees. A broad expanse of meadow in front has two men, one reclining and the other standing and pointing. A tree hangs into the top left corner, framing the image, its darkness reinforcing and defining the castle's light colour

78 Shanbally Castle – Doorway

A cart, with donkey and driver, is in front of the entrance porch of the Castle with two men, those seen in no. 77 above, standing facing it. They would seem to have the air of estate workers rather than owning the estate.

79 Anner Castle.

Anner Castle, the ivy-clad family home of the Mandevilles in the background with, framed by a tree, a family grouping of women and children arranged on the grass.

80 Kilmanahan Castle.

Kilmanahan Castle overlooking the quiet River Suir with the trees on the opposite bank reflected in the still water.

[119]Ex.681

[120]Differences (1) The frontispiece, with printed title, is of Holycross Abbey. This is in contrast to the museum copy which has *'Cloictheach on the Rock of Cashel'* as a frontispiece. The print, showing a woman in a light coloured dress, dark jacket and hat holding a bag was taken at the same time as the stereoscopic illustrations as the same woman appears in one of them (Hemphill 1860, View of Arch in Cemetery field).

(2) Unlike the museum copy, initial capitals and foliage decoration are not coloured.

(3) The stereographs are bound in at the back, not after each section of text as in 1983.350.

(4) The image titles, in red, are pasted on unlike 1983.350 where they are printed onto the page.

(5) Images are again pasted onto pre-printed frames with a monograph but the frame is slightly different.

(6) The monograph is smaller than that in 1983.350. There were therefore at least two printings of the pre-printed frames for stereographs. A third version, with a different form of foliage is visible on the card of a stereoscopic view of the gateway to Melview, a house in Clonmel (Ex.642, no. 8).

(7) A close comparison of the images in the two books shows that Ex.681 is missing many images. It may be that this copy was heavily used, perhaps with the pages removed for viewing and then trimmed and rebound.

[121]No.3 *'Panoramic view of Cashel, from the Rock'* in 1983.350 seems to have been replaced by *'General View, North-East- Rock of Cashel'*. This is a new view which is very similar to no. 2 *'General View North-East Rock of Cashel'* but does not have a gentleman seated in the foreground and has been taken closer to the Rock without the stone wall and with a row of poplar-like trees.

No. 7 is present but labelled slightly differently as *'West View Rock of Cashel'* rather than *'South-West View, Rock of Cashel'*.

A view similar to Number 11 in 1983.350 but taken at a greater distance from the nave is present before no. 8 and labelled as *'Eastern Nave and Remains of Window, Rock of Cashel'*.

Nos. 9,10,11 are missing and no. 12 is similar (to that in 1983.350) but a different image, taken from slightly further inside the building (the rim of the window embrasure is visible). The titles of no. 12 differ slightly also. Then come a number of earlier views, probably bound in out of sequence when rebound

No. 61 The Geometric garden differs slightly in that there are several people, nearly all women apparently on the pathway in comparison to 1983.350 where there are only five.

No. 67 *'Marlfield from the River'* differs also in that 1983.350 has a long distance view of the house with the river between and a coach and coachman on the near bank. The Ex.681 view is much closer, taken from the same side of the river with a man lying on the grass.

No. 68 'Croquet Ground, Marlfield' is different also with a view taken from slightly further away, a garden seat on the left and a different arrangement of people.

[122]Some of them are:

8   'View of Remains of Eastern Window and Choir'. The three views differ, one volume has a view similar to 1983.350 while two are closer to the east end of the Cathedral with people in view.

27   'Lismore Castle – East'. Two of the views are similar but the third is a more distant view of the same face of Lismore Castle.

28   'Lismore Castle and Bridge', two views are similar while a third is a far view.

29   'Lismore Castle, through the Entrance Gateway'.

30   'View from Drawing-room Window'. Two volumes have the view of the bridge while one is of the gardens only.

31   'View of Cathedral Spire from Carlisle Tower'. Two volumes have this view while one is different .

32   'View of Lismore from the Mitchelstown Road'. Again one volume differs by not having any people in the view

38   'Cahir Castle and Bridge'. Here there is a different view of Cahir as compared to 1983.350.

42   The Swiss Cottage shown with different people posed in front.

50   Again differences with the Model School Clonmel shown but only two of the books have ladies, St. Luke's and St. Joseph's in view

51   While two have the same view of the Railway Station, track, engine and worker, one has a view of the exterior of the station.

53   'View of Clonmel from the Heywood Road' with again differences in that one has field and a tent, but the others have a field and people with houses in the background, apparently as in 1983.350.

62   'Sir Thomas Osborne's Bridge, River Suir'. One of the three prints has two trees in it, the others not, taken from a different viewpoint perhaps.

76   'Shanbally Castle'. The three volumes show three different views of the castle.

79   'Anner Castle'. One album, presented to his daughter, has a different image of the same building compared to the other two.

[123]While the contents of some family albums contain work by both WDH and May Hemphill, it is clear from her albums that her work was not to the same meticulous and artistic standard as his. Her topics include family, Oak Ville, Old St. Mary's church and scenes around Clonmel and also records of ships, (Melampus and Gitana), and places (Ardcandrisk, Co Wexford (see Furlong and Hayes 1987, 163) and Botanic Gardens, Glasnevin) seen on trips taken with her father in the 1890's to Dublin and Wexford.

[124]The slide was prepared by Sanger, Shepherd & Co. of 5, 6 & 7 Gray's Inn Passage, Holborn, London. This has been described as ' a commercial product, c. 1906, could not be earlier than 1899. Probably made as a transitory process between the early process (3 gelatines dyed into 3 separate colours) and the later 3-in-one inhibition process. Process could be an combination of dye transfer printing and cyanotype printed direct onto a sheet of glass. So the sandwich would

be composed of the cyanotype image on glass combined with a sheet of gelatine containing the image of yellow and magenta produced by the inhibition process (the gelatine absorbs the two dyes selectively). From written opinion, source unknown, accompanying slide

[125] Family scrapbook

[126] Some years ago the County Museum acquired a small bound volume (Ex.552) with a green cover with boards, green spine with title 'Clonmel Art Exhibition' and five bands of Greek step pattern, all in gold leaf. Within it are three items

1 **Official Catalogue of the Clonmel Art Exhibition in connection with a collection of Works of Decorative Art from the Government Museum at South Kensington exhibited in Clonmel, 1858.** Printed by Edmond Woods, 1858.

2 **Address on Photography delivered on Thursday evening, September 30th, 1858 by W. D. Hemphill Esq., M.D.** Reprinted from the Clonmel Chronicle by Edmond Woods, Clonmel 1858.

3 A HMSO guide, **Catalogue of a Collection of Works of Decorative Art being a selection from the Museum at South Kensington Circulated for Exhibition in Provincial Schools of Art by J.C. Robinson, F.S. A. March 1858, Sixth Edition.**

The flyleaf is signed and dated William D. Hemphill, October 14th 1858, possibly the date when he received the book back from the binder.

Bound in between the Hemphill lecture and the HMSO catalogue are the following eight photographs (there may have been more as at least one page between them has been torn out):

1 Rectangular print, reproduction of an original oil painting of a white horse, a man and woman, dogs and other animals standing in front of a stone building with a gateway, doorway and Tudor-like mullioned window. Identified in ink below as No. 23 Loc. Cat. This painting is listed there as 'Watering, 1855' by J. F. Herring Senior, shown by Joseph White, Esq.

2 Rectangular print, reproduction of a print showing a pre-Raphaelite-like mother and child in a wood, 'No.199. Loc. Cat.' The corresponding entry, from the photographs section of the catalogue is '199 Copy of Engraving W.D.Hemphill'.

3 Rectangular print, reproduction of an original oil painting, a portrait of a young woman with curling hair, 'No. 19 Loc. Cat'. identified as 'Portrait of a Lady by Sir Thomas Lawrence' shown by Colonel Phipps, Oaklands, Clonmel.

4 Stereo pair, rectangular with rounded upper corners, 'No. 227 & c Gov. Cat' showing several pieces of Sevres porcelain on display in the Government case

5 Stereo pair, square with rounded upper corners, showing a general view of the 'Government Case' with framed works of art on the opposite wall and artefacts on the mantelpiece over a fireplace.

6 Stereo pair, square with rounded upper corners, showing the 'Local Case' containing a large number of small artefacts with several framed items hanging on the walls of the room.

7 Stereo pair, rectangular, landscape format, 'Frame P. Gov. Cat.' showing plaster casts of ivory 'bacchanalian subjects of Amorini or Cupids.....original ivories in the South Kensington Museum'

8 Single small print, domed top, showing a darkly dressed couple embracing, entitled 'Les Hugenots from a painting by Millais'. This does not appear to be noted anywhere else in the exhibition catalogue and it is possible therefore that it is not by Hemphill. However I

believe that all the images in the catalogue are by him and were taken during the exhibition.

[127]A Season Ticket to the exhibition is in the collection of the County Museum (1990.394). The committee is a list of the notables of Clonmel with strong representation from the Church of Ireland community and the Mechanics Institute. The Mechanics Institute had a School of Art, under the supervision of the South Kensington (now Victoria and Albert) Museum since 1854 (Ahern 1991,160). Among the committee were John Bagwell, M.P. Bernal Osborne M.P. and Henry Pedder. The art exhibition consisted of a large number of items, mainly paintings but also photographs, statuary, various items of craftwork and a miscellaneous section that includes some historical, Asian and ethnographical items. A large number of art works were displayed with many coming from notable houses in the area, few of which would have their original contents today. Edwin Hayes and Thomas Roberts are contributors with works of their own among them. WDH contributed six paintings to the display, three by James Harwood, one a view of Clonmel and all dated to the 1830's –1840's. The exhibition does not seem to have been well attended as WDH regrets that more people had not taken advantage of the opportunity to copy the works on display. This problem of the Mechanics Institute not actually attracting many mechanics or working class persons was one that recurred throughout the institution's history (Ahern 1991).

[128]Mr. Skaife, an avid experimenter in miniature photography is an important figure in the history of early photography (Schaaf 1983).

[129]Claudet and Mayall were both very successful professional society portrait photographers.

[130]Hemphill 1860, x.

[131]Mealys auction catalogue for Tuesday, Dec. 3rd, 2002, includes an image of the 'West Gate, Clonmel' (Lot 429) identified as by WDH. The apparently unposed nature of the people in the photograph would suggest it is an early image.

[132]As always we are subject to the accidents of survival and discovery.

[133]Heyert 1979, 141

[134]'Jaccord' and 'Miss V Sauss' (Ex. 640 small album associated with Newtown Anner)

[135]Sieberling 1986, 4-5.

[136]Dodier 1999, 30-1.

[137]Weaver 1989

[138]The maiden with the mirror, Dodier 1999, 48,

[139]The opinions in the preceding few lines are those of the late M.A. Keating of Clonmel, veteran photographer.

[140]Two unattributed photographs shown were a view of Venice (from Col. Phipps) and a portrait of Mr. Duane, late Secretary, United States of America, a native of Clonmel (from Captain Chaloner).

[141]Clarke 1997, 57

[142]Lloyd 1988

[143]the light, the window, the mirror and the young girl or woman –often dressed in white' (Lawson 1997, 9)

[144]copy letter, file 16/9 TSCM, Dodier to E. Earle, 8th August, 1999.

[145]The Royal Photographic Society, Bath holds the Amateur Photographic Association Albums. The contributing photographers were identified by numbers, WDH's is 198.

There are three Hemphill views in the albums (copies are in the collection of the South Tipperary County Museum).

STCM 1996.191 RPS 22609 view of Two Mile Bridge (seen elsewhere EC Album 1 as *Two Mile Bridge, River Anner, 1863*)

STCM 1996.192 RPS 22613 still life, Study of Flowers (seen elsewhere EC Album 1 as *Dendrobium Chrysanthum, 1862,*)

STCM 1996.193 still life , (titled EC Album 1 as *White Currants*)

[146]Chandler 2001, 40.

[147]

Great Exhibition London	Honourable Mention	1862
Amateur Photographic Association	Honourable Mention	1863
Amateur Photographic Association	1st Prize Gold Medal	1864
Amateur Photographic Association	Honourable Mention	1864
International Exhibition Dublin	Prize Medal	1865
International Exhibition Dublin	Do. for Interior Specified	1865
Amateur Photographic Association	Silver Cup	1865
Amateur Photographic Association	Honourable Mention	1865
London Photographic Society	Specially Mentioned by Jury	1865
Amateur Photographic Association	Silver Cup	1866
Amateur Photographic Association	Honourable Mention	1866
International Exhibition Paris	Certificate of Honor	1867
Amateur Photographic Association	Honourable Mention	
Amateur Photographic Association	Prize Coffee Pot	

[148]Chandler 2001, 41-2.

[149]EC Album 1, 34.

[150]Chandler 2001, 74.

[151]Copy in TSCM file 16/9.33

[152]Slightly different copies of this page of comments, varying in type face and in the addition of the Irish Builder's comments, are to be found in various copies of **Stereoscopic Illustrations** in family possession (EC album 9 and others) I am also grateful to Mr. Joe Walsh of Cahir for having provided me with a copy of the review in the Dublin Builder of 1st October, 1860.

[153]An interesting aside is Dermot Bolger's mention of WDH in his novel A Second Life, London, 1994, 177, ' I turned over an old photograph of the pond in Summer. The name W.D. Hemphill was stamped on the back with the date 1897. There were notes about the marsh plants….'.

[154]e.g. McGrath 1983, 1985. There was also apparently an article by David Brittain in the Amateur Photographer in 1982 but I have not been able to trace it as yet.

[155]Murray, K.A. (ed.) and Clemens, R.N. 1985.

[156]O'Connell (1985, 124-5). He identifies the river as a canal and the lamplighter, probably incorrectly, as the earliest photographed Irish workman.

[157]Sexton (1994, 28-9).

[158]Dodier (1999, 24). She reproduces 'Our First Drawing Room 1867' as illustrating this point but this image is of two of the Castletown Cox family and is not, strictly speaking, a tableau as it is a record of the two girls' entry into society and the dresses they wore on the day.

[159]Bence Jones 1996.

[160]Girouard 1992, 121-134. The family and carriages outside the front door, *View from Drawing*

Room, Newtown Anner, *1864*, The Slope *1862*, View from Dark Walk, Drawing Room, Newtown Anner. This publication is drawn from two earlier articles in County Life (Girouard 1988).

[161]Chandler (1989, 25-6).

[162]O'Donnell (1999)

[163]O'Dwyer (2001)

[164]Chandler (2001, 34-38)

[165]Portrait on the inside front cover of the photographic album of Old St. Mary's

[166]Ryan (1890, 135).

[167]Clonmel Chronicle, May 13th 1871, reference to Lismore Art Exhibition (I am grateful to Mrs . Shirley Duffy for this information.

[168]This image previously published, among others, by Sexton (1994.29) as 'Lady Blessington's Bath a well known boating pool in County Tipperary. Note the British Union Flag on the boat. Dr. William Despard Hemphill, c.1865. Albumen print from a wet plate negative'.

[169]Previously published (O'Connell, 1985 124) as 'Probably the earliest photograph (c.1860) of an Irish person at work on the canal at Clonmel left to us by an enthusiastic amateur. Dr. William Despard Hemphill (from Clonmel) was awarded a medal at the Paris exhibition for his photographs of local scenery'

[170]Bence-Jones (1996, 211)

[171]Robertson (1994,197)

[172]Girouard (1992, 127 and 1988, 227)

[173]Osborne (1870, Vol. One, 285)

[174]It might also be one of a number of young female artists from local Big Houses. Among them was Fanny Currey of Lismore Castle who exhibited a drawing 'The Laurel Walk at Newtown Anner' at the 1871 Clonmel Art Exhibition (Clonmel Chronicle May 13th, October 25th, 1871, information courtesy of Mrs Shirley Duffy). WDH may have received his artistic training in these circles.

[175]Courtesy Mr. David Griffin, Director, Irish Architectural Archive, Dublin.

[176]Herbert (1988, 130).

[177]Morris (1992, 310).

[178]Newtown Anner Album in private possession, image no.25

[179]Glin, Griffin and Robinson (1989, 136)

[180]Bence-Jones, (1996, 185)

[181]Glin, Griffin and Robinson, (1989, 24-6)

[182]O'Dwyer (2001)

[183]Obit.

[184]Ormsby (1888, 371)

[185]New Commercial Directory

[186]St. Mary's Church records, Clonmel, and succeeding references

[187]Slater's Directory

[188]Chandler Collection, National Photographic Archive.

Bibliography

Anon., 1966   'Irish Provincial Directories 1788-Directory of the Six Towns in Tipperary, by Richard Lucas' **The Irish Genealogist**, Vol. 3 no. 11, October.

Ahern, M.,   1993,   'Clonmel Grammar School' J. **Tipperary Historical Society**, 1993, 128-134.

Ahern, M.,   1991,   'Clonmel Mechanics Institute' J. **Tipperary Historical Society**, 1991, 159-162.

Basset, W, 1881   **County Tipperary Directory**

Basset, G.W., 1889,   **The Book of County Tipperary**, Dublin (reprinted 1991)

Bence-Jones, 1996,   **Life in an Irish Country House**, London.

Bence Jones, M., 1978   **Burke's Guide to Country Houses**, Vol. 1 Ireland.

Butler, P., 1990   **Three Hundred Years of Irish Watercolours and Drawings**, London

Butler, P. 2000   **Irish Botanical Illustrators and Flower Painters**, Woodbridge.

Burke, A. P., 1904   **A Genealogical and Heraldic History of the Landed Gentry of Ireland**, tenth edition, London.

Chandler, E. and   **Through the Brass Lidded Eye, Photography in Ireland,**
Walsh, P.   1989   **1839-1900**, Guinness Museum, Dublin.

Chandler, E., 2001   **Photography in Ireland: The Nineteenth Century**, Dublin

Clarke, G.   1997   **The Photograph,**   Oxford.

Coe, B., 1976   **The Birth of Photography**, London.

Crookshank, A., and   **The Watercolours of Ireland**, London.
Glin, Knight of, 1994.

Cusack, J.1984   'The Oak Ville Story', **The Nationalist**, 31st March, 1984

Davison, D.H. 1989,   **Impressions of an Irish Countess**, Birr.

Devine, J. 1989   **Down the Great Road: a Journey to Lemonaghan**, Dublin.

Dodier, V., 1999,   **Clementina, Lady Hawarden**, London.

Ellwood, C.V. and 'The Lady Blake Collection: Catalogue of Drawings of Jamaican
Harvey, J.M. V 1990 Lepidoptera and Plants' , **Bulletin of the British Museum (Natural
History) Historical Series** , Vol. 18 No. 2, 145-202.

Furlong, N.   **County Wexford in the Rare Oul' Times, Vol. 2**, Wexford
and Hayes, J, 1987

Girouard, M. 1988 'Newtown Anner, Co Tipperary', **Country Life** September 8th
         180-185, September 15th , 226-231.

Girouard, M. 1992 **Town and Country**, New Haven and London.

Glin, the Knight of, **Vanishing Country Houses of Ireland**, Dublin, 2nd
Griffin, D.J. and   Edition.
Robinson, N.K.1989

Guinness D, and   **Irish Houses and Castles**, London
Ryan, W., 1971

Guy, F., 1886   **Directory of Munster**, Cork

Guy, F., 1893   **Directory of Munster**, Cork

Richard, P. M.1988 'Life in Three Dimensions: The Charms of Stereoscopy' in **A New
History of Photography**, ed. M. Frizot, Cologne, 175-183.

Haworth-Booth, M **The Golden Age of British Photography 1839-1900** New York
1984 (ed.)

Hayes, J. C., 1989 'Guide to Tipperary Newspapers' **J. Tipperary Hist. Soc.** 2, 1-16.

Hemphill, W.D.   **Address on Photography Delivered on Thursday Evening,
1858   September 30,1858**, printed by Edmund Woods, Clonmel
         (reprinted from the Clonmel Chronicle).

Hemphill, W.D.   **Stereoscopic Illustrations of Clonmel, and the Surrounding
1860   Country including Abbeys, Castles and Scenery**, Dublin.

Hemphill, 1875   'Examination of Minute Bloodstains in Medico-Legal Investigations'

	Dublin Journal of Medical Science, Vol. LIX, April, 330-334).
Henry and	'General Directory of Cork, Cork.
Coughlan, 1867	
Herbert, D., 1988	Retrospections of Dorothea Herbert 1770-1806, Dublin
Holland, P., 1999	'A Portrait of Cornwallis Maude', **Tipperary Historical Journal**, 1999, 140-144.
Howitt, W., 1864	Ruined Abbeys and Castles of Great Britain and Ireland, London.
Heyert, E., 1979	The Glass-House Years: Victorian Portrait Photography 1839-1870, London.
Kinder, F., 1839	**The New Commercial Directory for the cities of Waterford and Kilkenny and the towns of Clonmel, Carrick-on-Suir, New Ross and Carlow'** Kilkenny
Killanin, and	**The Shell Guide to Ireland**, Second Edition, London.
Duignan, M.V.,	
1967	
Lawson, J. 1997	Women in White: Photographs by Clementina Lady Hawarden, Edinburgh.
Lee, J.J., 1994	'Introduction' in Sexton, 1994, **Ireland, Photographs 1840-1930**, pp 7-11
Lloyd, V., 1988	Roger Fenton: Photographer of the 1850's, London.
Long, B., 1999	**Tipperary S.R. County Council 1899-1999: A Century of Local Democracy,** Clonmel.
Mealy, 1995	Important Fine Art Sale on the Premises at Ballinaparka, Aglish, Co. Waterford, Tuesday, September 5th, 1995' Castlecomer,
Mealy, 2002	Sale of Rare Books, Manuscripts, Maps and Ephemera, Etc, Tuesday, December 3rd, 2002' Castlecomer.
Murray, K.A. (ed.) and	
Clemens, R.N.1985,	'An Early Photograph' **J. Irish Railway Record Soc.** Vol. 15, no. 98 Oct.
Nelson, E.C. and	**The Brightest Jewel: A History of the National Botanic Gardens,**
McCracken, E.M.	**Glasnevin, Dublin,** Kilkenny.

1987,

Nelson, E.C. 2001   Review of **Irish Botanical Illustrators and Flower Painters** by Butler
(2000) in **Irish Arts Review Yearbook 2002**, 215-6.

McGrath, W., 1983   'Precious Volume Years Ahead of its Time' **Evening Echo,** Cork,
14th March and 'Ireland's Earliest Loco. Photo', 11th July.

1985   'Wonders of Early Photography' **Evening Echo,** Cork,
30 th January.

Morris, H. F., 1992   "The 'Principal Inhabitants ' of County Waterford in 1746"
Waterford History and Society, Dublin, 309-330

Obit.1   'The Death of W. D. Hemphill, Esq., M.D., F.R.C.S.I.' **Clonmel
Chronicle,** n.d. reprinting obituary of 16th July, 1902 and account
of funeral dated 19th of July, 1902

Obit. 2   'Death of Dr. W.D. Hemphill' **Nationalist,** 16th July, 1902.

O'Connell, M., 1985   **Shadows; An Album of the Irish People, 1841-1914** Dublin, 1985.

O'Donnell, S., 1999   **Clonmel 1840-1900: Anatomy of an Irish Town,** Dublin.

O'Dwyer, F., 2001   'A Noble Pile in the Late Tudor Style' : Mitchelstown Castle
Irish Arts Review Yearbook 2002, vol. 18, 30-43.

Osborne, C.I. 1970   **Memorials of Lady Osborne,** two volumes. Dublin.

Ormsby, L.H. 1888   **Medical History of the Meath Hospital,** Dublin

Quinlan, M., 2001   'Architecture' in **Old St.Mary's presents a Festival of
Flowers, Souvenir Programme,** July 2001.

Robertson, P. 1994   **The New Shell Book of Firsts,** London.

Ryan, C.A., 1890   **Records of the Tipperary Artillery,** Clonmel

Rynne, C. and   'An Early Photographic Study of the Eighteenth
Wigham, B., 2002   Century St. Fin Barre's Cathedral' **Journal of the Cork
Historical and Archaeological Society,** 107, 199-210.

Scarry, J., 1997   'Victorian Images of the Past', **Archaeology Ireland,** Vol.11,
no.3, 20-21.

Schaff, L. 1983   'Thomas Skaife's Pistolgraph and the Rise of Modern Photography in
                         the Nineteenth Century' **The Photographic Collector**, Vol. 4 no. 1
                         Spring, 27-39.

Seiberling, G., 1986   **Amateurs, Photography and the Mid-Victorian Imagination,**
                         Chicago.

Sexton, S., 1994,   **Ireland, Photographs 1840-1930**, London.

Sexton, S., 2002   **The Irish, A Photohistory 1840-1940**, London

Stalley, R., 1985,   'The Original Site of St. Patrick's Cross, Cashel' **Nth. Munster
                         Antiq. J.** xxvii, 8-10,

Weaver, M., 1989,   'Roger Fenton: Landscape and Still Life' in **British Photography in
                         the Nineteenth Century:The Fine Art Tradition,**
                         Cambridge, 103-120